Philosophy of Cruelty

Collected Philosophical Essays

by

Giorgio Baruchello, PhD

NORTHWEST
PASSAGE
Books

Gatineau, Quebec, Canada

Philosophy of Cruelty

Collected Philosophical Essays

by Giorgio Baruchello, PhD

ISBN: 978-09939527-5-3

Published by
Northwest Passage Books
Gatineau, Quebec, Canada

Cover photo: Arch doorway, formerly of a bank in downtown Ottawa, Canada, installed in the Mackenzie-King Estate, Gatineau Park, Quebec, Canada. Photo by Brendan Myers.

This book is dedicated to all victims of bullying,
an insidious and pervasive form of cruelty,
at all ages and in all places:
human life painted in ugly colours.

Contents

Preface

In the attempt to disseminate and spur philosophical reflection beyond sole academic circles, scholarly conferences and professional periodicals, Northwest Passage Books has offered me once more the opportunity to collect, revise and polish several past works of mine, which were written and published between 2000 and 2015. After a first volume focussing upon the philosophical theme *par excellence*, i.e. mortality, I was invited to gather and reshape articles, discussion pieces and book chapters, all of which deal with a less commonplace philosophical theme: cruelty. As the issue of mortality had led me into the history of philosophy, the lethal consequences of deficient conceptions of economics and the insights of a select group of great thinkers, so does the theme of cruelty open an equally rich spectrum of topics for keen philosophical inquiry. Fittingly, I explore here: (1) the most frequent conceptions of cruelty in Western culture; (2) some controversies surrounding its understanding in politics and in ethics; and (3) the contemporary school of political thought that is based upon its explicit and forceful rejection in the public sphere, championed by Judith Shklar and Richard Rorty, and known as *liberalism of fear*. I write "explore" because this is what the book consists in, chiefly: visiting strange new places, namely diverse thoughts and systems of thought, without knowing in advance where the wandering mind may end up. This book does not preach, though it does not shy away from judging, at times. It does not build a neat structure, though it organises a great variety of building blocks. Rather, this book sails over the vast sea of the Western canon and, while drawing a map of the same, it identifies the most perilous areas and the ones with fish aplenty.

Mortality terrifies and nevertheless intrigues many people for its inescapable yet definitive, indeed life-defining, character. In an analogous way, cruelty both repels for its intrinsic ugliness and yet appeals to a *fond noir à contenter* [a dark depth to please] that most persons experience not infrequently within their own psyche, as exemplified by the broad allure of crime novels, horror movies and the eager morbid curiosity elicited by car crashes along the busiest motorways. Possibly because of the resulting ambiguity at the heart of cruelty, which is both revolting and fascinating, philosophical works about cruelty are both sparse and ample. On the one hand, when one reviews the philosophical and theoretical literature, she discovers that there exist very few studies devoted entirely and explicitly to it. Long monographs and large tomes on cruelty are particularly rare, unlike voluminous inquiries into, say, knowledge, justice, or government.[1] On the other hand, remarks and considerations about cruelty abound in studies dealing with cognate terms (e.g. violence, oppression, vice) and related phenomena that affect social relations nearly everywhere in the world and at a considerable variety of levels (e.g. education, crime, statehood, law enforcement, sexuality, agribusiness, healthcare). The material and the ideas presented in this book should be of interest to the reading public at large, for we all are bound to meet cruelty in our lives at some point. We may not like the idea and even less the experience, but there is often nothing that we can do about it, as some of the following chapters make clear. Also, the same material and ideas should be of interest to those academics that have not come across the past studies of mine hereby collected and re-edited, since they have obvious and obviously significant implications for sociology, criminology, psychology and legal studies. Northwest Passage Books and its chief consultant, Dr. Brendan Myers, dare cross the border separating academic and non-academic publishing, in order to let many disciplines and mental attitudes criss-cross and cross-fertilise. In the same spirit, I hope to be able to reach a most diverse readership and stimulate reflection in all departments—academic ones, yes, but above all, of human life.

Acknowledgments

I wish to thank wholeheartedly, once again, Dr. Brendan Myers, chief consultant at Northwest Passage Books, for encouraging me and helping me to combine and refine my previous work on cruelty into one book. A dear friend of mine and a fellow graduate from the University of Guelph, his contagious entrepreneurial spirit, his appreciation of my research and his genuine intellectual curiosity made the present volume possible. This book is the second instalment in a collaborative project that, in our intentions, should continue in the future and lead to an expansion in the catalogue and in the readership of Northwest Passage Books. Above all, our joint hope is to engage a philosophically inclined readership that does not orbit primarily or solely around the gargantuan industry of academic publishing, which is often self-referential, self-secluding and, eventually, self-defeating. Therefore, I must thank warmly and sincerely the editors and the publishing houses of the academic books and scholarly journals in which my studies on cruelty were previously made public. In an age of jealous for-profit copyright enforcement like ours, not even the authors of a published piece of research can be sure to retain full control over their own creations. Fortunately, the editors and publishing houses with whom I had to deal in connection with this volume proved both helpful and prompt in their positive response.

Noteworthy is the support that I received from the editors of *Appraisal*, the journal issued by the British Personalist Forum (formerly Society for Post-critical and Personalist Studies), namely Drs. Simon Smith and R.T. Allen. No fewer than five chapters in this book contain materials published by *Appraisal* between 2003 and 2007. Likewise, I must express my gratitude to the rector and the senior management of the University of Akureyri for granting me a sabbatical leave in the academic year 2016–2017, during which I could devote myself to a hefty number of research projects, including the volumes penned for Northwest Passage Books. Dr. Enrico Albanesi and Prof. Carlo Penco of the Università degli Studi di Genova should be thanked too: for their kind friendship first; and secondly for allowing me to access with ease key facilities at their university and for providing me with precious office space. My family in Italy should be thanked as well for adding an even more precious item to the mix: longer time to write. Finally, I wish to pay a special homage to the co-authors of some of the texts re-drafted and re-issued in this book: Drs. Antonio Casado da Rocha of the University of the Basque Country, Colin D. Pearce of the University of South Carolina, and Wendy C. Hamblet of North Carolina A&T State University. It is through open dialogue and lively exchange that true depth and breadth of thought can be attained. All three co-authors were most generous on both accounts. Their knowledge, insightfulness and expertise inform and enrich enormously this book, and most definitely its first part. Nonetheless, though benefitting immensely from their proficiency and collaboration, if any imprecision or error is to be found in the pages that follow, then the responsibility lies exclusively with me. Whilst success is an exciting cooperative enterprise, failure is a sad and lonely business.

Introduction

Thanks to the interest of Northwest Passage Books, I bring together in this volume five journal articles, two conference papers, one book chapter, an obituary, and five discussion pieces. Some of these works are fairly informal, others are thoroughly academic, two are relatively personal. All these texts were written between 2000 and 2015, though one of them is still awaiting publication in the second volume of the *Yearbook of the Law Faculty of the University of Akureyri*, which is going to be issued with considerable delay since its scheduled release date, two years ago. Differences in publication date, typology, length and style aside, what all these works of mine share is their focus-point: *cruelty*.

In part one of the book ("Debating Cruelty"), I assemble and re-work thoroughly five discussion pieces variously co-authored with Drs. Wendy C. Hamblet, Antonio Casado da Rocha and Colin D. Pearce for the British philosophy journal *Appraisal*, plus another one co-authored only with Dr. Casado da Rocha for the now-defunct Spanish journal *biTARTE – Revista cuadimestral de humanidades*, and a related article issued by the Dutch journal *Bijdragen. International Journal in Philosophy and Theology*. The discussion piece from *biTARTE* required translating most of the text back into English, the original drafts being no longer available to either of its authors and the official Spanish version being of little use to the readers of the present volume. To a significant extent, I 'took over' the old co-authored discussions and streamlined them here into coherent book chapters, whilst retaining the slender, dialogical and lighter character of the original publications. Through these works, duly re-drafted: (1) the most salient theoretical connotations of cruelty are introduced to the reader; (2) the most widely discussed ethical and political implications of cruelty are presented succinctly (especially with regard to liberalism); (3) the chief conceptions of cruelty by significant thinkers (especially Nietzsche and Levinas) are outlined briefly; and (4), as a result, the stage for further reflection is established firmly, especially with regard to themes that are tackled in greater detail in the rest of the book.

In part two of the book, "Cruelty in the History of Thought", I re-issue three broad philosophical vistas on cruelty that can help the reader to gain a more precise sense of the most frequent conceptions of this notion in Western culture. The first vista is comprehensive and synthetic, for it stretches from classical antiquity to the 21st century, and identifies five recurrent interpretations of cruelty in Western thought. The second vista deepens the analysis of one of them, as this particular vista is embodied in the work, if not in the personae themselves, of two controversial European philosophers and literati, i.e. Donatien Alphonse François, Marquis de Sade, and Friedrich Nietzsche. The third vista conjoins and contrasts a medieval interpretation of cruelty in the penal sphere, i.e. the Florentine poet Dante Alighieri's *per* [in accordance with] his *Divine Comedy*, and a modern one, i.e. the Norwegian criminologist Nils Christie's. This essay is actually based on research that I had pursued in my graduate days for my PhD thesis, entitled *Understanding Cruelty: From Dante to Rorty*, which was successfully defended at the University of Guelph many years ago. *Qua* [as] independent essay, however, it was put together much later, in view of a 2015 *Festschrift* [celebratory collection of essays upon a special occasion] in honour of Prof. Mikael M. Karlsson of the University of Iceland.

As the second part of this book is concerned, I must add that my first volume for Northwest Passage Books contains a chapter that could and perhaps should have been included in it, but was not. I am referring to chapter 7 of *Mortals, Money, and Masters of Thought*, entitled "Cruelty and Austerity. Philip Hallie's Categories of Ethical Thought and Today's Greek Tragedy". I decided to utilise it in my book about death and mortality because, in that chapter, I survey and assess the austerity policies implemented in Greece after 2008 at the behest of the so-called "Troika" as a stark token of the lethal character of mainstream yet mistaken conceptions of economics. Bad economics kill people; and they do so cruelly, at times, as explained in that chapter. However, Hallie's conceptualisation of cruelty remains canonical well beyond the tragic case of contemporary Greece. As such, even though his views are tackled in chapter 4 of this book, I nevertheless refer the reader to the previous chapter 7 as a useful thematic and conceptual bridge between my two volumes.

In part three of the book, named after the Latin phrase for "Deliver Us from Cruelty", I consolidate in three chapters five different texts about one specific school of political thought that, in the late 20th century, made cruelty central to the understanding of social and political life, claiming that Western liberalism is characterised by a unique abhorrence of cruelty in the public sphere. Called "liberalism of fear", this school of thought was an explicit creation of Judith Shklar, but it is commonly associated with the self-declared herald of stars-and-stripes neo-pragmatism, Richard Rorty, who was probably the most famous American philosopher at the end of the last century. Consistently, four of the five texts centred upon Rorty, who is still well-known in the present century too. As I pen this introduction, his name has re-appeared on the pages of many newspapers, at least in the Anglophone press, and some aspects of his political thought are going 'viral' across the world-wide-web. The philosopher who, exactly like Judith Shklar, claimed that "liberals... think that cruelty is the worst thing we do", had also remarked, back in the 1990s:[2]

Members of labor unions, and unorganized and unskilled workers, will sooner or later realize that their government is not even trying to prevent wages from sinking or to prevent jobs from being exported. Around the same time, they will realize that suburban white-collar workers—themselves desperately afraid of being downsized—are not going to let themselves be taxed to provide social benefits for anyone else... At that point, something will crack. The nonsuburban electorate will decide that the system has failed and start looking around for a strongman to vote for—someone willing to assure them that, once he is elected, the smug bureaucrats, tricky lawyers, overpaid bond salesmen, and postmodernist professors will no longer be calling the shots... Once the strongman takes office, no one can predict what will happen. [However, o]ne thing that is very likely to happen is that the gains made in the past 40 years by black and brown Americans, and by homosexuals, will be wiped out. Jocular contempt for women will come back into fashion… All the resentment which badly educated Americans feel about having their manners dictated to them by college graduates will find an outlet… [e.g. in] socially accepted sadism… directed toward people such as gays and lesbians[.][3]

To past Continental generations and probably most contemporary historians, a socio-political picture like the one portrayed above is likely to recall autocratic demagogues such as Napoleon III and Benito Mussolini. When examining the same passage, however, today's US, Canadian, Australian or British readers, and therefore today's journalists and opinion-makers in English-speaking countries, cannot but think of Donald Trump. Fresh US President and long-time billionaire, he won in 2016 a harsh electoral campaign against a seasoned politician, Ms Hillary Clinton. Throughout the campaign, Mr. Trump: (1) uttered racist, sexist and homophobic slurs; (2) fashioned himself *qua* anti-establishment champion of the impoverished, economically insecure, and primarily white working class of his country; (3) paraded his willingness to cooperate with foreign dictators and political leaders whose human-rights record is far from spotless; and (4) insouciantly condoned words and concepts that make violence, torture included, seemingly acceptable in the public sphere, both domestically and internationally.[4] Cruelty, in the shape of "socially accepted sadism" or worse (e.g. extensive warfare), might then regain the front stage as a major ingredient in the political life of the world's sole nuclear super-power, whose 500 and more military sites outside US borders and territories span across most continents, and *a fortiori* [all the more so] in the political life of all countries at large.[5]

On the other hand, the new US presidency might prove less prone to endorse the highly destructive forms of legally termed humanitarian intervention and politically proclaimed promotion of Western-style democratic institutions seen, say, in 21st-century Libya, Iraq and Afghanistan under George W. Bush and Barak

Obama (e.g. military occupation, air raids and killings by remote-controlled drones). On the domestic front, Trump himself might succeed in becoming an effective tribune of the common people, or at least of a large segment of it. Chronically disenfranchised blue-collar Americans might end up enjoying more and better jobs than they have over the previous three decades. Who knows? They might even witness the end of the gross if not grotesque imbalance in incomes and influence between Wall Street and Main Street that Ronald Reagan's economic policies kick-started in the 1980s, and that Bill Clinton's 1999 repeal of the 1933 Glass-Steagall Act definitively entrenched. Rather than christening involuntarily a shantytown, as some of his predecessors did (i.e. post-1929 "Hooverville" and post-2008 "Bushville"), the name of a flamboyant US billionaire might go down in history for reverting the forceful re-affirmation of patrimonial capitalism that has been occurring in most countries on Earth since the days of Thatcherism. Alternatively, as Rorty suggests in the same foreboding pages of *Achieving Our Country*, the elected "strongman" will just "make peace" with "the international super-rich" and appease the masses *via* [by means of] jingoistic militarism and charismatic posturing. Time, as always, will tell. Cruelty, in any case, is never too far away, if we only wish to look.

Original publication credits

As already done *vis-à-vis* [with regard to] my first book for Northwest Passage Books, I revised in this volume several older publications of mine, in order to ensure consistency, avoid or reduce redundancies, update some references, insert useful chronological information, explain foreign-language phrases and borrowings in contemporary English that some readers might not be entirely familiar with, and eliminate the occasional linguistic oddity, misprint or plain error that had survived prior editorial reviews. Overall, the modifications were kept to a minimum, even if I was seriously tempted to change thoroughly my older texts in light of my current insights, inclinations and interests. Only on four occasions did any substantial re-writing take place, i.e. chapters 1–3 (because of turning polyphonic, fragmented discussion pieces into monophonic, coherent book chapters), 3 again (because of re-translation from Castilian into English and merging with a scholarly journal article), and 8 (because of the merging of three thematically related essays into one chapter). In these four cases, chapter titles that are conspicuously different from those appearing in the original publications flag out the substantial re-writing of the older texts occurred in the present volume (only minor changes were made to the titles of chapters 4, 5 and 7, whilst those of chapters 6 and 9 are identical). Again, chapters 1–3 are based upon texts co-authored with other academics, to whom I am greatly indebted. The full details of the old publications are as follows (please note that they are not reiterated later in the book):[6]

Chapter 1
What is Cruelty?, *Appraisal*, 5(1), 2004, 33–8 & 56; and Is Violence Always Cruel?, *Appraisal*, 5(2), 2004, 91–4 (both with Dr. Wendy Hamblet).

Chapter 2
Discussion on Cruelty (with Drs. Colin Pearce, Wendy Hamblet and Antonio Casado da Rocha), *Appraisal*, 5(3), 2005, 135–43 & 159; and On Cruelty and Nietzsche's Drive to Distinction (with Dr. Colin Pearce), *Appraisal*, 5(4), 2005, 187–9 & 199–200.

Chapter 3
Debate on Cruelty (with Dr. Antonio Casado da Rocha), *biTARTE – Revista cuadimestral de humanidades*, 27, 2002, 5–22; and Cesare Beccaria and the Cruelty of Liberalism. An Essay on Liberalism of Fear, *Philosophy and Social Criticism*, 30(3), 2004, 303–13.

Chapter 4
No Pain, No Gain. The Understanding of Cruelty in Western Philosophy and Some Reflections on Personhood, *Filozofia*, 2, 2010 (section A. "A View beyond the Frontier"), 170–83.

Chapter 5
The Politics of Cruelty: An Essay on Sade and Nietzsche, *Appraisal*, 4(4), 2003 ("Two papers from the 2003 Appraisal/Polanyi conference"), 165–74.

Chapter 6
Ordinary Hell. Reflections on Penal Justice between Dante and Nils Christie, *Ársbók lagadeildar Háskólans á Akureyri* 2(1), forthcoming (due 2015).

Chapter 7
Disciplinary Divisions and Petty Academics: Three Reminiscences and One Rumination in Memory of Richard Rorty (1931–2007), *Appraisal*, 6(4), 2007, 25–30.

Chapter 8
Richard Rorty: A Sophist without a Soap-Box, *Agora*, 19(2), 2000 ("Notas"), 139–52; Rorty's Painful Liberalism, *Bijdragen. International Journal in Philosophy and Theology*, 63(1), 2002, 22–45; and Irony and Its Limits. An Essay on Richard Rorty, *Appraisal*, 4(3), 2003 ("Other papers"), 127–31 & 137.

Chapter 9
Enemies of Interculturalism. The Economic Crisis in Light of Xenophobia, Liberal Cruelties and Human Rights, *Nordicum-Mediterraneum. Icelandic E-journal of Nordic and Mediterranean Studies*, 10(2), 2015, <http://nome.unak.is/wordpress/volume-10-no-2-2015/c81-conference-paper/enemies-of-interculturalism-the-economic-crisis-in-light-of-xenophobia-liberal-cruelties-and-human-rights/>.

PART I – Debating Cruelty

Chapter 1: Two Questions about Cruelty

Question 1 – What is Cruelty?

In his celebrated *Pensées* [Thoughts], Blaise Pascal (1623–1662) stated that we have three fundamental sources of belief: reason, intuition and tradition.[7] In order to formulate an answer to the question at issue, we must refer to all three sources. My first step, then, is to pursue the third source of belief by reviewing succinctly a selection of representative statements about cruelty by famous philosophers from the origins of Western thought to the late 19th century.[8] My second step is to determine whether and, if any, which intuitions their views on cruelty inspire, address or rely upon. Finally, Pascal's first source of belief can help us to evince a reply to the interrogative at issue, thanks to the information resulting from the previous two steps.

Ancient, Medieval and Early-modern Views

Aristotle (384–322 BC) is said to have condemned cruelty as "calculated acts of outrage" and, for this reason, as morally worse than "acts committed in anger".[9] Lucius Annaeus Seneca (4 BC–65 AD) censures it too as "the inclination of the mind toward the side of harshness".[10] For him, exemplarily cruel are "those who have a reason for punishing, but no moderation in it".[11] In this, they differ from those displaying "savagery... who find pleasure in torture"; about such a bestial disposition, he quips: "we may even call it madness".[12] Similar is the position of Thomas Aquinas (1225–1274), who defines cruelty as "hardness of the heart in exacting punishment"; it is not to be confused with mercilessness, i.e. inadequate pity when pity is due.[13] Cruelty is a form of "human wickedness", for it involves reflective deliberation and, in this, it differs from "savagery" and "brutality", which are forms of irrational "bestiality" feeding on "the pleasure [some people] derive from a man's torture".[14] First to deviate openly from this choir of disapproval is Niccolò Machiavelli (1469–1527), who, in *The*

Prince, mentions "cruelties being badly or properly used… and the possibility of evil… to speak well… [i.e.] of those [cruelties] that are applied at one blow and are necessary to one's security, and that are not persisted in afterwards unless they can be turned to the advantage of the subjects".[15] Against Machiavelli's quasi-utilitarian justification of cruelty resonates Michel de Montaigne's (1533–1592) dismissal of the same, for "cruelty" possesses a morally dubious parent—"fear is the mother of cruelty"—and equally dubious children: "chastisements", "hunting", "torture" and "war".[16] Indeed, with regard to war, in which he was obliged to participate as a sworn vassal of the French crown, Montaigne writes disdainfully: "I could hardly be convinced, until I saw it, that there were souls so monstrous that they would commit murder for the mere pleasure of it… For that is the uttermost point that cruelty can attain."[17] A witness to the English Civil War, Thomas Hobbes (1588–1679) follows Montaigne in his loathing of warfare, as he states that "to hurt without a reason tendeth to the introduction of war, which is against the laws of nature, and is commonly styled by the name of cruelty".[18] 'Montaignesque' sounds also Joseph Butler (1692–1752), who claims that "disinterested cruelty is the utmost possible depravity, which we can in imagination conceive", although he believes it to be a very rare phenomenon.[19]

Enlightenment and Romantic Views

In his belief of cruelty's empirical uncommonness, Butler is echoed by David Hume (1711–1776), who doubts that even "the cruelty of Nero be allowed entirely voluntary, and not rather the effect of constant fear and resentment".[20] Charles-Louis de Secondat, Baron de La Brède et de Montesquieu (1689–1755), on the other hand, finds cruelty to be much more widespread and to imply a very important point in favour of penal moderation. In fact, Montesquieu identifies an entire nation that is affected by endemic "cruelty", i.e. Japan, *qua* dramatic effect of the relentless use of inhumane punishments in that country: "True is that the character of this people, so amazingly obstinate, capricious, and resolute as to defy all

3

dangers and calamities, seems to absolve their legislator from the imputation of cruelty, notwithstanding the severity of the laws... [A]re such men, I say, mended or deterred, or rather are they not hardened, by the continual prospect of punishment?"[21] Still, penal moderation has to be... moderate, at least according to Adam Smith (1723–1790), for whom "mercy to the guilty is cruelty to the innocent".[22] After all, Smith himself cannot afford to be too kind-hearted, since in the free-trade economy that he praises, "there is no order that suffers so cruelly... as the race of labourers" whenever commerce declines—a necessary evil for which he sees no human remedy.[23] In Smith's opinion, cruelty is therefore not a rare event. Quite the opposite, it is part and parcel of the economic order upon which the wealth of nations depends. Even less rare is cruelty according to Jean-Jacques Rousseau (1712–1778), who, in his *Confessions*, lists as "cruel" or "cruelties" such diverse, painful or disquieting phenomena as remembrances, agonies, uncertainties, separations, lost affects, diseases, hands, oppressions, errors, offences, calumnies, deaths, imaginations, inconveniences, and even idleness itself.

Perhaps, in his *Confessions*, Rousseau implicitly confirms the Marquis de Sade's (1740–1814) understanding of "cruelty" as "nothing but the human energy that civilization has not yet corrupted... Cruelty, far from being a vice, is the first sentiment that Nature has imprinted within ourselves. The child breaks his toy, bites his nurse's nipple, strangles his bird, long before he has reached the age of reason."[24] Dreadfully widespread is cruelty, if we pay heed to Giacomo Leopardi (1798–1837), who envisages "the cruelty of punishments that are common in the State" as well as the cruelty of philosophy and religion, because of which "humankind... look now upon death not as the end of their miseries, but as that after which more unhappiness has to come... [Not only philosophers and priests] have been crueller to the human being than fate or necessity or nature... but... have surpassed in cruelty the most ferocious tyrants and the most ruthless executioners ever seen on Earth."[25] In addition, human "neglect and indifference [are] the cause of an infinite number of cruel and vicious actions", which must therefore be added to the dismal score.[26] Indeed, the whole of life seems to be pervaded by cruelty and the only consolation for "the strong man [is] to see, with stoical gratification, all of destiny's cruel and hidden cloaks being stripped off".[27] An admirer of Leopardi, Friedrich Nietzsche (1844–1900) embraces super-humanly this tragic realisation and defines "cruelty... as one of the oldest and most indispensable elements in the foundation of culture... the psychology of conscience is not, as is supposed, 'the voice of God in man', but the instinct of cruelty".[28] In Nietzsche's view, "almost everything we call 'higher culture' is based on the spiritualization and deepening of cruelty. The 'wild animal' has not been killed off at all; it is alive and well, it has just – become divine."[29] According to him: "Cruelty is one of the oldest festive joys of mankind... for to practise cruelty is to enjoy the highest gratification of the feeling of power", which, in Nietzsche's view, is the fundamental drive of all things human.[30]

Fastidious Distinctions and Distinctive Features

To conclude, as far as concerns the Western philosophers just surveyed, the concept of cruelty is by no means univocal. It refers to deliberate, excessive violence, to irrational, bestial sadism, and to indifference to another's suffering. It excludes direct and/or indirect justified exercises of violence and it includes them. It is blatantly bad, but it can be used well for the common good. It is a rare condition, yet it is most ordinary. It is a prerogative of the human being, although it can be described as an all-pervading metaphysical force. Most puzzlingly, all connotations touch upon intuitive dimensions of cruelty, whether existential, moral, or historical. Some cruelty is certainly contained in phenomena such as: the dark arts of the executioner; the eruptions of unrestrained physical violence; the refined tortures of the libertine; the daily experiences of humiliation and abuse of the prisoner; the premeditated, cold uses of political assassination; the ordinary struggles of each and every one of us against death, illness, need, frustration, disillusionment, rejection. Perhaps, rather than speaking of one cruelty, it would be more appropriate to speak of, and discern amongst, many a cruelty.[31]

Trying to sort out such a seemingly equivocal collection of conceptions, a first distinction could be drawn between 'natural' cruelty and 'human' cruelty. The former would refer to the understanding of cruelty as a fundamental energy embedded within the universe itself, which does find expression in human agency, i.e. in the latter type of cruelty, but not exclusively.[32] This latter type of cruelty could be divided itself between that which stems from 'delight' in another's suffering, and that which stems from 'indifference' to another's suffering; this suffering being determined either by the 'action' or the 'inaction' of the perpetrator.[33] Action and inaction, in turn, can operate 'directly' and/or 'indirectly', i.e. along a short or long chain of moral responsibility.[34] Finally, cruelty of the 'human' type could be divided into 'orthodox' cruelty and 'unorthodox' cruelty, depending on whether it is morally, legally, religiously, customarily and/or otherwise justified, or not. As one progresses from one distinction to another, however, the reply to "what is cruelty?" translates more and more into replying to another question, i.e. "which cruelty is there?"

This perplexing translation does not mean that we cannot retrieve any common denominator, though. After all, we are still talking of various types of the same thing, i.e. of cruelty. We may be at odds trying to define it, but we generally know cruelty when we see it. Besides, defining concepts, including ordinary ones or those by which we lead our lives, has never been easy: just think of justice, beauty, truth and intelligence, for example.[35] To retrieve a common denominator, we must look at very general features, shared by most of the cruelties listed above, or at least a set of family resemblances. The first and most evident is *suffering*: there must be detriment of some kind resulting from the form of human and/or natural agency that we label as "cruel". The second feature is the *actuality* of the agency that brings about the suffering, and of the suffering itself: if the detriment of somebody is only hypothetical, then there is nothing but cruel intentions or a mystification of cruelty. The third feature is the presence of some *mens rea* [culpable mind], whether human or non-human. Somebody, or something, is responsible for the suffering, whether by direct or indirect action or by omission,

6

displaying either delight in or indifference to the suffering she/it causes. Even in the cases of 'natural' cruelty there seems to be some sort of *mens rea* involved, which has been variously described as God's evil mind, Nature's callous indifference to our destiny, or even the personification of the social order under capitalism as a collective, Freudian, anal Oedipus.[36]

The Eye of the Beholder

We can indeed look to the opinions of any number of thinkers, the usages in any number of contexts, to determine what is being meant when the term "cruelty" is employed. This investigation, as briefly demonstrated above, cannot but open onto a universe of meaning, a veritable Pandora's box for the one chasing down a firm definition. It is interesting to notice, in regard of the plethora of meanings for the term "cruelty", the way in which it comes into view for the subject (the one controlling the definition) only from the safe distance of the observer of the cruelty *of others*.

That is to say, it becomes a far easier affair to select "calculated acts of outrage" and "forms of irrational bestiality" when others are the agents of those behaviours, than when one is oneself entering into activities that may be so characterised. When we look at actions that are undeniably cruel—the experiments of the Nazi doctors, the hacking of Tutsi neighbours by Hutu individuals during the Rwandan genocide, the terrorism of Timothy McVeigh, the "collateral damages" of American retaliatory bombings in Afghanistan and their "war of liberation" in Iraq—we find that, even in these extreme acts of bloody brutality, cruelty, like beauty, resides in the eye of the beholder. People very rarely see their own actions as cruel. Sociopaths and bullies are often blind to the havoc and to the immense suffering that they cause. In fact, the number of perpetrators who enjoy committing acts that could be named cruel are few. On the contrary, it seems to be the case that people are often physically disabled at the prospect of having to hurt, maim or kill others. We have reports of Nazi infantrymen, whose orders included shooting in the back of their heads civilians lying face down on the ground. The soldiers could not, for vomiting or passing out, fulfil their tasks of executing the innocent prisoners (the ineffective executioners would then simply be shuffled off to desk jobs, exposing the flimsiness of other executioners' arguments that there was a kill-or-be-killed policy among the soldiery in Nazi Germany). Few people see their own actions as cruel. They may regard them as unfortunate necessities or as the lesser of evil options available at the moment, but they rarely see themselves as cruel persons for having committed the acts that others might call "cruel". In truth, many of the worst perpetrators are fully convinced that they are doing good when they are harming other people. Witness in the world today how many acts of mass murder, how many episodes in the "War on Terror", cite their particular god as not only condoning, but demanding the brutality. To understand the purity that is felt at the home-site of cruel action, we may have to refer, once again, to the philosophical tradition.

Plato (428–348 BC) has insisted, with his mentor Socrates (470–399 BC), that no one knowingly does wrong. All moral error is an epistemological problem and not an evil choice made in calculated coldness.[37] That explains why early education is so important for Plato that the just city is declared an improbability unless it begins with citizens ten years of age or younger. If people's understanding is not given shape well enough soon enough, there is little hope that their adult lives will be led morally. For Aristotle, too, moral behaviour is about knowing the correct response to situations as they arise, and this knowingly correct response can only be developed through the healthy repetition that builds moral habit, as well as by choosing one's friends and exemplars with care.[38] Phenomenologists in the post-Holocaust tradition are also stunningly accepting of the notion of the essential innocence of cruel perpetrators. Emmanuel Levinas (1906–1995), whose extended family was lost to the Nazi genocide and who himself spent the war years in a Nazi prison camp, has affirmed this Socratic claim. No one does harm knowingly. As Levinas shows in his phenomenological account of the lived experience of human subjects, each subject, through pleasure and use, "unthinkingly" goes about her business of carving out a safe house in the voluptuous real of the "elemental", and though all subjective encounter is fundamentally violent—all acts being appropriative—the violence entailed in all human encounters is "innocent" because "unknowingly" effected.[39] This includes, for Levinas, the cruel "irresponsibility" of the SS guards.[40] In a stunning hyperbolisation of the call to responsibility (encapsulated in the divine charge to be 'the brother's keeper'), Levinas makes the suffering victim responsible even for the guard's irresponsibility.[41] Levinas states:

> *Biology teaches the prolongation of nourishment into existence; need is naïve. In enjoyment I am absolutely for myself. Egoist without referent to the Other; I am alone without solitude, innocently egoist and alone. Not against the Others, not 'as for me...'—but entirely deaf to the Other, outside of all communication and all refusal to communicate —without ears, like a hungry stomach.*[42]

If all action is fundamentally violent and yet innocently (unintentionally) effected, then cruelty, being a subset of violence where intention (to harm beyond the demands of just punishment) takes on particular importance, ceases to exist. No act can be cruel, no agent of any monstrous act can be cruel, if subjects are "naïve" and oblivious of the harm that they do—"entirely deaf to the Other".

In everyday parlance, when we speak of "cruelty", we mean to denote people or acts that have to do with deliberate excessive violence. People may be cruel by either performing cruel acts or by entertaining and acting upon cruel intentions. The cruelty seems to reside in the intention to do unwarranted (because immoderate) harm beyond the necessities of well-intended punishment. Cruel intentions subdivide into two main categories—where the agent exhibits pleasure in harming; or where the agent is indifferent to the harm that she effects onto others. Where there is pleasure in harming, we may safely use the term "pathological" and admit its rarity. Where there is indifference, we have a graver problem: we must admit that almost everyone has the potential for cruelty. When refugees panicked and fled the Nazi Regime in the spring of 1939, nine hundred odd mainly Jewish refugees took to the seas in the MS *St. Louis*.[43] Everyone had landing certificates illegally sold to them in Germany by the Cuban Director of Immigration. When the landing certificates were invalidated upon entry into the Havana harbour, the refugee ship was ordered out of Cuban waters. US histories love to cite this cruel rejection of those so desperate, but rarely do they mention that the ship sailed on to Florida, then to Canada and back to Europe, and was consistently turned away at every port. No one would aid them in their plight. Finally, Britain came up with a plan to share the refugees among several countries and Britain, France, Belgium and Holland each took a portion of the homeless victims. No doubt, few of the citizens of those hard-hearted countries who had turned away the refugees would characterise themselves as cruel, yet their indifference was a crucial factor in the problem. Had they cared for their human fellows in their time of need, perhaps the end-result in human lives would have been more positive. Only 350 of the 936 refugees that returned to Europe survived the Nazi terror.

The Vast Fields to Behold

Many thinkers, from Joseph Butler to Roy F. Baumeister (b. 1953), have written that cruelty is rare.[44] But, if cruelty can be the fruit of indifference, then almost every person on the planet is cruel —most certainly those of us in the West who have access to certain knowledge about the suffering masses on Earth and go on with our lives in complete obliviousness to the fact of their misery. Indifference to the woes of other human beings is an almost universal human feature. Otherwise how is it the case that, with thousands of children dying each day from hunger and hunger-related diseases, the world has not gone mad with compassion [Lat. *cum* (with) + *patior* (to suffer)] in the suffering-with of these vast masses of innocents? The vastness of the suffering masses echoes the vastness of the semantic area covered by "cruelty". Indeed, my historical survey could retrieve only very general features of the concept at issue. Generality, however, is not necessarily a bad thing.

Generality is only one step behind universality, which is a target at which many philosophers have aimed, whenever they have seriously tackled the critical understanding of metaphysical, ontological, epistemic and ethical categories. In this respect, one further general element is added by the hermeneutical shift away from "the cruelty *of others*" and onto an evaluative perspective: cruelty does seem to reside "in the eye of the beholder".

Depending on whose role and relative position that we consider within the context of a phenomenon, the acknowledgment of cruelty may be more or less straightforward. In fact, due to cruelty's necessarily adversarial two-party nature, which comprises the perpetrator and the victim, two major potential accounts compete for recognition, one for each party involved. Whenever the account of the perpetrator is 'louder', the term "cruelty" itself is likely to disappear from the scene as an applicable moral category; unless the perpetrator is an honest sadist, who is willing to admit that cruelty is exactly that which is being brought forth by her. Too much blameworthiness, shame and disapproval are implied by "cruelty" for most people to be prone to predicating it of one's own actions (and/or inactions). Whenever the victim's account is 'louder', instead, then "cruelty" is likely to persist and to connote most forcefully the dramatic two-party interaction at stake. Most tellingly, the typical first step in a person's and/or group's struggle in opposition to the cruelty that is being perpetrated against them is the obtainment of full recognition as victims of cruelty. Crying, calling the police and writing newspaper articles are all possible means to this morally important end.

The shift onto an evaluative perspective should not be taken as an ethical scandal, or as a reason for epistemic discouragement. No form of knowledge can subsist without an initial interpretative angle, no matter whether it is personal, collective, self-serving or instrumental. From this interpretative angle one can select, evaluate and define the meaningful 'bits' of reality to be dealt with and understood as specific phenomena—without a point of view, there is nothing to be viewed. Of course, such an interpretative angle needs not to be absolute and unchangeable, even when it is apprehended tacitly by all the members of a certain community throughout most of their existence—given a point of view, another can be taken. A rigid body of reference is also required to apply the categories that were tacitly and/or explicitly endorsed, thus allowing the fundamental and indispensable lexicon of the knower to be employed consistently—without a stable body of reference, the view cannot but be blurred. Once again, this body of reference needs not to be the only one available, and it may be cognitively and/or morally relevant to change it, so as to cope with phenomena for which our lexicon appears to be inadequately equipped—a bright, well-defined and terse view may keep too much out of view. Philosophers, scientists, political theorists, moralists and the moral agent as such are all in one and the same position. They may possess and/or agree upon a set of fundamental categories, which they can apply rationally if and only if they adopt a specific body of reference, which serves as a standard of comparison for any further evaluation. Personal experiences, cultural backgrounds and differences of character can all have an influence in the determination of this body of reference. One, however, must be selected, lest the categories possessed remain inapplicable. As regards the two-party context of cruelty, this body of reference is most likely to be either the perpetrator's account, or the victim's. As stated before, the former tends to deny that cruelty applies as a relevant moral category *vis-à-vis* her own actions (with the notable exception of the candid sadist), whereas the latter tends to do the opposite. The conclusive evaluation of the context may be formulated eventually by either of the two parties involved, or by a third party: a 'neutral' observer.

Still, even in the case of a 'neutral' observer, the issue boils down to deciding whether the victim's claim that cruelty is the case is correct or not. Prudential reasoning suggests that the victim's account be preferred always and anyway: if cruelty is dreadfully bad, as agreed upon by most thinkers and by common sense, then we ought to try to avoid cruelty as much as possible. Hence, whenever there may be somebody claiming to be the victim of some cruelty, we would better refrain from acting, or from non-acting, as not to reinitiate and/or continue the alleged cruelty. Naturally, prudence can lead to seemingly paradoxical consequences. For example, teenagers would never go out dancing not to be cruel to their overprotective mothers. Analogously, as odd as it may sound to some of us, private corporate companies would not be taxed by any 'rapacious' or zealous public authority, in order for these authorities not to be cruel to the companies' stockholders. By following prudence, we are likely to encounter variously and problematically competing claims of cruelty, if not even actual paradoxes. In such cases, the only solution may be to opt for lesser evils. Giacomo Leopardi had already suggested this solution in his works, since he depicted the human condition as a painful, endless picking amongst misfortunes (pleasure itself being nothing but momentary respite from pain). The present brief philosophical survey points in this dramatic direction too, for we are reminded of how much cruelty exists that is due to sheer indifference. Instead of seeing cruelty as a rare, almost insane reality, we may have to acknowledge instead the tragic ordinariness of cruelty. No morally competent living person is not involved in some causal chain of action (or inaction) leading to the detriment of another. No morally competent living person does not realise that she is also morally responsible for it in some degree. No morally competent living person does not become aware of the fact that trying to change one's own position along such chains of action (or inaction) may cause new and/or further detriment to oneself and/or to others. What shall we do? Which chains should be broken? And which kept?

It is precisely to find an answer to these questions that philosophical thinking is required. Common sense can give us a valid foothold whence to start. However, common sense cannot lead us all the way to the solution of moral quandaries. To achieve this goal, we need a deeper and better sense of the value basis allowing us to assess the nature and the extent of the detriment that is caused by the various cruelties, among which we are compelled to choose. Also, prior to that, we need a clearer understanding of the specificity of cruelty, for this moral category cannot but be vague, as long as we have not been able to distinguish it better from its most common semantic cognates, such as aggressiveness, brutality and, in particular, violence. Perhaps, the results of philosophical thinking will be equally unable to solve the quandaries *in toto* [completely]. Still, such results are likely to have taken us farther than mere common sense. The final solution is bound to be left to the wisdom that moral agents mature in their life. Like all moral agents before and after them, we all are called to exercise the ever-changing and context-specific art of applying practically our own theoretical understanding of the universe in which we dwell and act.

Question 2 – Is Violence Always Cruel?

In Aristotle's distinguishing "calculated acts of outrage" as examples of cruelty (*contra* [against] "acts committed in anger"), he gives us a classic definition of cruelty that is clearly still with us today in the West. Here, cruelty is located as a subset of violent actions where cold calculation sets the agent apart (as morally worse) from those committing violent acts when merely blinded by passion. Calculation speaks to the (perhaps prior) intention to commit the outrage, rather than the less culpable violent act resulting from the momentary loss of clarifying practical reason. However, many philosophers have insisted that more than cold calculation is at work when cruelty happens. For an action to be named truly "cruel", there must be, beyond cruelty as embedded in the intent, a certain pleasure in the suffering of the other, or at the very least indifference to that suffering. Thus, the question "is violence always cruel?" could be answered with a clear negative. Violence is not always cruel; only that violence where evil intention causes a compassionless or delighted response to the suffering of the undeserving innocent, or to an exaggerated, immoderate degree or form of suffering applied to those deserving punishment.

A Matter of Perspective

Empirical evidence testifies to the fact that certainly violence happens and, often, where these distinguishing characteristics are not

14

to be found. If we hold to this narrow definition of cruelty, then many everyday actions that involve the violation of the rights and bodies of others begin to look like little more than well-intended corrective measures or, at their most extreme, thoughtless accidents. Parents regularly violate the rights and bodies of their children, but, having the child's moral education and sometimes the child's safety as the intent, the parent cannot be named "cruel", according to a narrow definition. However, if cruelty is defined in terms of the intent and (compassionless) response *in the agent*, then we run the risk of missing some of the subtlest and most painful cruelties quite evident from the perspective *of the victim*. If the intent remains pure, and the agent of the violence remains caring in regard of the victim, we seem condemned to exonerate our perpetrator as merely accidentally or inappropriately violent, instead of outright cruel. Yet, commonplace gut reactions tell us that this exoneration is misplaced. A personal example reported to me might help to clarify the chief concern here.

When teaching an ethics class centred about discussions of "Home and Violence" in a fundamentalist Christian pocket of the Central Valley of California, the teacher who reported this tale was approached by a troubled and nervous, often incoherent young female student of hers. She stayed after class one day to confide to her that her religious convictions were somewhat ambiguous. On the one hand, she understood the God of Christianity in the image of a loving and just father, ready to forgive his children their sins. On the other, at a young age, she had been taught by her earthly father to beware the 'just deserts' of sin, when he held a flaming lighter under her forearm and explained through her screams: "If you think this hurts, imagine what hell feels like." Assuming that the father in question considered this method of behaviour modification to serve the best interests of his daughter's moral progress, the working definition of cruelty employed here requires that we name this treatment of the child's body (and her sense of security and well-being) mere violence, unintended as genuine harm. What I am suggesting by raising this counterexample to the definition of cruelty applied here is that the breadth of abstract definitions may have a direct bearing upon the actions that agents undertake. Acts of violence happen as a matter of course in the world. We frighten our children into safe conduct around roads, strangers, and Halloween candy. Police violate our rights when they pull us over and check our licenses on a whim. Security agents at the airport are paid to routinely de-humanise travellers, rummaging through their personal effects, having them stand in lines bereft of their footwear and warm outer clothes. But these possible violences, whether seemingly minor or not, are far from those of the student's father, though his intentions may have been purer than any of these other perpetrators. Since broader definitions of violational behaviours may serve to limit those very behaviours, it is crucial that cruel behaviours be named as such, and with the widest breadth that reasonably fits.

Emmanuel Levinas' Perspective

This concern explains why some philosophers, especially those thinking in the post-Holocaust world, have chosen to hyperbolise their characterisations of violence to radicalise our moral sensitivity, even in the case of inadvertent violations of others. For example, Emmanuel Levinas broadens the definition of violence to include all acts of representation. According to him, "knowing" is itself a kind of appropriation where the subject takes up a one-sided view of the object and represents that single aspect or "side" as the whole of the object; for Levinas, others are radically "other", their differences from my "known" extending into the depth of infinity beyond the "side" that is appropriated as "known by me".[45] This means that we must understand even our most loving relationships to be appropriative in structure, grounded in 'my use' or 'my pleasure' of the loved one. The relationship is, at the very least, *potentially* violent, if not necessarily so. Levinas' broadening of the definition of violence almost *ad absurdum* [to absurdity] is meant to alert the agent to the ease with which the best intentions can permit, and perhaps even cause us to slip away, conscience-free, into violent behaviours. Levinas may disappoint many careful etymologists by going too far with his definition of violence.

However, in another regard, Levinas goes not far enough in naming the spade a spade. In an essay entitled "The Ego and the Totality", Levinas attributes all violent behaviour to egos that are merely "unthinking".[46] The violation of others cannot be remedied, in this essay, but at least the violator can learn to be aware of the harm that she effects in the world by becoming a "thinking being", aware and taking care, and acting "under apology" with regard to the others around her.[47] And elsewhere, in a shocking exoneration that we have already encountered, Levinas insists that an agent of violence is to be understood as merely an "innocent egoist and alone… not against the Others, not 'as for me…' but entirely deaf to the Other, like a stomach that has no ears."[48] We must admit, then, that, while Levinas has a keen sense of the potential for violence embodied in every relationship, he is far too generous in regard of the agents of violence. No agent, in his account, comes off as outright cruel. The worst culprit is simply morally impaired, not yet a "thinking being". While his account of the violence of loving relations may offend our sense of intimate connection, his insistence that all egos are merely as innocent as hungry stomachs flies in the face of what we witness to be empirically evident in the world, with each new war of aggression, each new King Leopold II or John C. Osgood, not to mention murderous tyrants like Hitler and Stalin. Many people—even parents, husbands and children, idealistic leaders and religious icons, even where driven by the best intentions, even where compassionate for the objects of their acts in the world —can be simply, ordinarily, yet unthinkingly cruel.

In our everyday parlance, we condemn as cruel those agents or events that involve intent to harm and compassionless response to the harm that is caused. By this definition, some of the most wanton acts of violence slip by as merely unintentional or well-intended errors. On the other hand, if we take very seriously the criteria for cruelty employed thus far, it can be argued once more that we must name "cruel" all well-fed, well-sheltered citizens of the First World. In a world where each and every day between 25,000 and 36,000 innocent children die of hunger and hunger-related diseases while grain rots in our fields, where we in the West enjoy an ecological footprint that grants us forty times our fair share of the world's resources, where wars of political and economic aggression are celebrated as acts of heroism when levied by the richest of nations upon the poorest and most defenceless of Third-World countries, where the victims of those wars are no longer just its soldiery but seven out of eight of their victims are now innocent civilians, it is difficult to deny that cruelty can come in many guises, including the 'innocent' acts of violence of omission that permit us good conscience in the midst of such a world. We can well be culpable because we are comfortably dispassionate about the overwhelming vastness of global misery.

The Evaluative Perspective

Even by defining "cruelty" in the very loose way suggested in the beginning (i.e. upon the basis of actual suffering brought about by an agent who displays delight in or indifference to the victim's suffering), we may not have enough semantic 'substance' to cover all the existing cases of cruel behaviour. Whenever the agent's intentions are pure, as in the example of the harassing Christian fundamentalist father, cruelty may turn most perplexingly into something far less reproachable, such as well-intended corrective measures. In order to make sense of this puzzle, another element has to be kept in mind firmly, so as to understand why speaking of "cruelty" can result pragmatically/ethically problematical and how any unsatisfactory, partial account of potentially cruel behaviour can be properly integrated from a semantic/cognitive point of view: the perspective from which the action is being evaluated. Insofar as the agent's intentions are assessed from the agent's perspective, the alleged purity of the agent's intentions may cause "cruelty" to leave the scene *in lieu* of some slightly more acceptable "violence". This eventuality is, perhaps, morally irresponsible. However, it is not counterintuitive. It appears semantically/cognitively viable, insofar as it portrays the event(s) to be assessed from a plausible angle of observation.

Equally plausible, but pragmatically/ethically more revealing, is the victim's perspective. This perspective makes "cruelty" much more resilient and much more unlikely to leave the scene. More than intention-guided, in fact, the assessment of the possible cruelty at stake is suffering-guided. The fact alone that the victim is suffering leads, so to speak, to the suspicion that cruelty is actually there. Prudential considerations require that the victim's accusations, rather than the agent's declared aims, be the starting point for the assessment of cruelty. If our ethical/pragmatic aim is the reduction and/or avoidance of cruelty, then the cognitive/semantic integration and/or substitution of the agent-based approach with the victim-based one is of fundamental importance. In short, the victim's perspective should be taken as often as possible, for it is the one that is more likely to minimise the probabilities for cruelty to arise and persist. This evaluative choice is contingent upon a prior commitment to the minimisation of cruelty, which is something that many agents may regard (though not declare openly) as secondary to other commitments, such as the maintenance of public order, the maximisation of money-returns, or the protection of personal freedom for self-realisation.

Still, even when the victim's evaluative perspective is taken, the intentions of the agent will not and cannot be relegated to some inferior level of consideration or excluded altogether. They pertain to the assessment of cruelty. Not to do so implies that any action bringing about suffering can turn into a cruel action, including my involuntary dropping a heavy hammer on your toes, or the dentist's unwelcome pulling of the wrong tooth of mine. Levinas' own broadening of the notion of violence, so as to include claims of knowledge themselves, hints at this possibility, which I consider metaphysically plausible but ethically perplexing, for it defuses the concern for violence by 'spraying' it onto all aspects of existence. It is not casual, perhaps, that Levinas ends up justifying the SS' criminal behaviour, for whoever lives appears to be bound to commit violence by living as such. Not to properly consider the agent's intentions is at least as counterintuitive as not to condemn the harassing Christian fundamentalist father as cruel. Moreover, by combining the consideration of the agent's intentions with the victim's evaluative perspective, it becomes more likely for the assessing party to realise whether the agent is actually:

[A] deriving hidden delight from the suffering caused by her action; or
[B] being *de facto* [in effect] indifferent to the suffering caused by her action.

One could sensibly argue that, to get back to the personal experience reported, were the father really caring and love-guided, he would look for less gruesome, alternative forms of soul-saving assistance for the daughter, at least and especially after hearing the daughter's screams of pain and discomfort. As for the claim that only the agent can be the judge of her own intentions, allow me to remark *en passant* [incidentally] that God, the juror, the therapist and the insightful partner may often have a better sense of what the agent meant to do when she did it, and be required to use it. Hence, most people would probably take into account the intentions of the father also in order to determine, at least, the degree of cruelty of the action that he performs, i.e. burning his daughter's forearm with the flame of a lighter, so as to remind her of the dangers of eternal damnation.

I cannot deny, however, that other people, and not necessarily only Christian fundamentalists, may want to insist in taking those very same intentions into account in order to determine whether the father was *really* cruel or not; that is to say, whether he was not cruel but, presumably, overzealous, stupid or unimaginative. Sadly enough, they would say, terrible things often follow from people's lack of understanding: of themselves, of other people, and of the consequences of their own actions. Levinas' justification of the SS guard's criminal behaviour on grounds of moral underdevelopment points exactly in this direction and forces us to wonder: can shallowness, ignorance and stupidity disqualify a claim of cruelty? Can any detriment due to mere causal responsibility (and not also to moral responsibility) be seen as cruelty? Are perhaps shallowness, ignorance and stupidity morally laden causal factors that we tend not to recognise as such?

Both State courts and Divine Justice (*per* the Christian tradition, at least) tend to distinguish not only the suffering caused voluntarily from the suffering caused involuntarily, but also the suffering caused voluntarily in the name of self-interest from the suffering caused voluntarily in the name of altruism. Are they right in doing so? And if they are right, are they tracing a dividing line between violence and cruelty, or just between more and less severe forms of cruelty? Under this respect, the less gruesome cruelties of the State mentioned above are far less excusable than the gruesome cruelty of the ignorant Christian fundamentalist. Unlike the latter, the former had time and resources, both material and intellectual, to conceive of alternative paths of action devoid or quasi-devoid of detriment.

Shifting evaluative perspective, thus individuating hidden sadistic streaks and actual brutality, may not solve all problems, though. Even when the victim's evaluative perspective is considered regularly before the perpetrator's, dilemmas may not cease to exist, and it may be still difficult to determine whether an action is truly cruel or not. After all, shallowness, ignorance and stupidity could be much stronger and much more pervasive than hidden sadism and actual brutality. Furthermore, the detriment itself of cruelty may be difficult to assess, as short-term detriments may produce long-term benefits, and short-term benefits, instead, long-term detriments. Being cruel *hic et nunc* [here and now] may prove good *a posteriori* [after the fact]. Using physically painful means *hic et nunc* may strengthen the moral character of the individual and maximise her chances to be a good citizen, or a good Christian. Not to mention the frequent experience whereby one feels forced to choose between cruelties of different degree, rather than between cruel and non-cruel paths of action. Such choices, as many of us have experienced in life, are never easy. Perhaps, in this inevitability, life itself proves to be inescapably cruel.

Concluding Remarks

To wonder seriously about the nature and most basic features of cruelty involves reflecting upon the deepest ontological and axiological assumptions of ours: can the concern for spiritual salvation, for instance, override the concern for physical well-being? When can we justify any intervention into another's personal sphere of freedom? And what kind of detriment is needed for cruelty to subsist? The present analysis must then move further, broadening and deepening its scrutiny, and I wish to suggest a series of interrogatives about cruelty to be tackled by the inquiring mind:

1. Can cruelty follow from shallowness, ignorance and stupidity?
2. What kind of detriment must cruelty entail in order to be real cruelty?
3. Can cruelty be good, at least instrumentally?
4. Can there be a universal notion of cruelty, in spite of differing ontologies?
5. Can existence (nature, life, the universe) be cruel?

I invite all the readers to try to find answers to these questions, insofar as they can help the moral agent or the assessing individual to determine when and whether cruelty is the case, and whether or when her own conduct is cruel. Some of them are tackled in the following chapters of this book. Probably, no all-catching definition of "cruelty" will be produced thereby, and no all-revealing gut reaction magically present within our souls will be discovered either. After all, people have kept and keep disagreeing about all sorts of claims of cruelty (and of justice, beauty, liberty, etc.). Still, the assessment of cruelty is a most important issue, at least in terms of practical wisdom, which requires the development and the cultivation of one's own *esprit de finesse* [Fr.; literally "spirit for fine things", i.e. insight, intuition, tacit powers of integration]. Moreover, were we really to believe that we can know always and for sure when and why cruelty is the case, then we would probably put ourselves very quickly in the position of the Christian fundamentalist father just presented. Such a man is very confident about his intuition about what is cruel (i.e. eternal damnation) and what is not cruel (i.e. the use of physical force for the sake of another's salvation). He knows violently, in Levinas' sense, and he teaches violently. Perhaps he teaches violence too, if not cruelty itself.

It should be noted that our sense or gut feeling for cruelty can be nurtured as well as suffocated, and it is most important for personal and interpersonal well-being that individuals are educated to recognise and act upon cruelty. This should be done with the same passion and efficacy with which ancient Icelanders were trained to regard pillaging and raping in the Hebrides as nothing worth reproaching. All aspects of the human psyche are involved in moral development. A reasoned understanding of cruelty is needed in addition to our ethically revealing gut reactions, which can alert us to important moral features of the world in which we live, as well as to the insights accumulated by philosophers and by intellectuals in the history of our civilisation, which we have merely outlined here and mused upon a little. Reason, intuition and tradition, as I derive from Blaise Pascal, form our imperfect yet sole weaponry in the struggle against the evils of cruelty.

Chapter 2: Three Perspectives on Cruelty

Perspective 1 - Psychology

The list of possible cruelties derived from representative philosophers in the previous chapter does not clearly suggest that striving to be at one's best, to do the right thing, or to be a virtuous person is in fact to practice a form of cruelty. Nevertheless, this is precisely the claim made by Friedrich Nietzsche in the thirtieth aphorism of his book *Daybreak*, entitled "Refined cruelty as virtue".[49] Here Nietzsche suggests that we should "not think too highly" of "a morality which rests entirely on the *drive to distinction*" (Nietzsche's own emphasis).[50] His thinking is that we should first ask ourselves "what kind of a drive" is it that seeks for distinction and what kind of psychology "lies behind it?"[51] And when we do find an answer to these questions, Nietzsche says, it will be that we wish to make others suffer. In seeking to "do our best", we are in fact seeking "to make the sight of us *painful* to another and to awaken in him the feeling of envy and of his own impotence and degradation" (Nietzsche's revealing own emphasis, again).[52] When we do someone the "supposed favour" of being complimentary and drop some "of *our* honey" (*ditto* [as said before]) onto "another's tongue", we are all the while "looking him keenly and mockingly in the eyes".[53] This is because "we want to make him savour the bitterness of his fate".[54]

The History of the Species

Nietzsche goes on to provide a few examples of good deeds or laudable conduct that illustrate the cruelty underlying our attempts to live up to the higher standards of virtue and excellence. If we see some person who "has become humble and is now perfect in his humility", then we should "seek for those whom he has long wished to torture with it!"[55] "[Y]ou will find them soon enough!" Nietzsche adds.[56] If someone is "kind to animals and is admired on account of it", then there must inevitably be "certain people on whom he wants

24

to vent his cruelty by this means".[57] The "great artist" is another exhibit in Nietzsche's gallery of cruelty, because of "the pleasure he anticipated in the envy of his defeated rivals".[58] It was the anticipation of this pleasure which he would feel in the envy of others that "allowed his powers no rest until he had become great... [H]ow many bitter moments has his becoming great not cost the souls of others!"[59] Even "the chastity of the nun" is nothing but this drive to cruelty.[60] It looks with "punitive eyes" into the faces of women "who live otherwise".[61] "[H]ow much joy in revenge there is in these eyes!" Nietzsche exclaims.[62] For Nietzsche, the "theme" of the cruel intentions underlying our efforts to be virtuous "is brief", but "the variations that might be played upon it might be endless".[63] Moreover, these many variations will not be "tedious" to us at this point, because it is "still a far too paradoxical and almost pain inducing novelty that the morality of distinction is in its ultimate foundation pleasure in refined cruelty".[64]

Nietzsche goes on to explain that he is not arguing that every action at every time by every person seeking to do their level best is motivated by the cruel desire to make others suffer. By the "ultimate foundation" of the morality of distinction, Nietzsche means this morality's "first generation".[65] This hypothetical first generation began the process of civilisation by becoming individualistic enough to seek recognition by others of their superior talents and virtues. However, individuals inherit "the habit of some distinguishing action" and yet they may not be behaving out of cruel motives. This is because "the thought that lies behind [the action] is not inherited with it (thoughts are not hereditary... only feelings)".[66] Provided that the feelings of cruelty behind these actions aimed at distinction and recognition are "not again reproduced by education", even so soon as "the second generation", there is a failure "to experience any pleasure in cruelty in connection with [them], but only pleasure in the habit as such".[67] This pleasure in simply doing the virtuous action out of habit and tradition is what Nietzsche calls "the first stage of the 'good'", which is to say the first stage of the attraction to human beings of the fine and the beautiful in itself without any thought of selfishness or self-love.[68] Nietzsche is explaining to us that although we ourselves might not be doing good for cruel reasons alone, at some point in the past our ancestors certainly were, and he traces the many cruelties expressed in the drive to excel to a common root in the psychological history of the species.[69]

Nietzsche focuses on the basic feature common to all forms of striving to do well or to do one's best, i.e. the anticipated pleasure in seeing one's rivals and other observers suffer under the knowledge that they have not likewise succeeded in doing these things, or that they lack the natural abilities to make even a passable try. He therefore highlights the suffering of the politician defeated in a close electoral race, the employee terminated by an arrogant boss, the student who is beaten by a classmate in a scholarship or athletic competition, or the academic who is denied tenure while his colleague receives it. His focus is not on those who have to deal with oppression, discrimination, violence, illness and despair. These examples of suffering no doubt remind us how cruel life can be, and certainly raise the question of 'man's inhumanity to man'. Nonetheless, they do not point the inquirer in the direction of the paradoxical conclusion at which Nietzsche wishes us to arrive, i.e. that our virtuous behaviour, at least in its deepest origins, is in fact rooted in a kind of egoistic malice, or a Iago-like craving to see others in pain. Following out the suggestion of Nietzsche's aphorism, we learn that there may be many forms and kinds of goodness or virtue evident in our efforts to impress other members of our species, but for all that there is underlying these various behaviours one unifying motive and that is the wish to make others suffer in some way. In this context at least, Nietzsche manages to make goodness or virtue multifarious and cruelty univocal instead. He is not entirely alone in this. Christian apologist William Paley (1748–1805), for example, says that he knows no "stronger stimulus to exertion" than "envy": indeed, "many a scholar, many an artist, many a soldier, has been produced by it".[70] However, "since in its general effects it is noxious, it is properly condemned, certainly is not praised, by sober moralists".[71] Thus Jesus censures "love of distinction and greediness of superiority".[72] To this point of Paley's we may add another from William Edward Hartpole Lecky (1838–1903):

> [T]he philosophies of ancient Greece and Rome appealed most strongly to the sense of virtue, and Christianity to the sense of sin... It is impossible to look upon the awful beauty of a Greek statue, or to read a page of Plutarch without perceiving how completely the idea of excellence was blended with that of pride. It is equally impossible to examine the life of a Christian saint, or the painting of an early Christian artist, without perceiving that the dominant conception was self-abnegation and self-distrust.[73]

In a nutshell, Nietzsche's understanding of human morality asserts that our ancestors aimed at virtue in order to rejoice in the painful humiliation of their neighbours. His study of cruelty is genealogical, grasping an initial factor of development of human morality that, according to Nietzsche's own account, is likely to have disappeared along the process of development. Not unlike teeth and fingernails, the "drive to distinction" may have been needed by the individual to defeat competitors in prehistoric or ancient times.

Today, however, the same drive seems to serve the goal of collective well-being. After all, teeth are used to smile and fingernails to pick sheets of papers fallen from a colleague's desk. Furthermore, even if smiles and acts of kindness may still be used to humiliate another, most typical virtuous behaviours *as such* are difficult to explain along Nietzsche's line of understanding, e.g. parental devotion to a new-born child and the stranger's assistance to a person in need, which have been observed even in other higher mammals since ancient times (e.g. dolphins). I must confess to the reader that I have serious doubts concerning the comprehensiveness of Nietzsche's claim, which is meant to disclose the basic feature common to *all* forms of striving to do well or do one's best. Without dwelling too much on the exegesis of Nietzsche's philosophy, I invite the reader to consider the possibility that Nietzsche's views may be the misshaped fruit of: (1) a social-Darwinist outlook, which detects selfish competition also when genuine cooperation is the case; and/or (2) a genial, highly creative but overstretched intellectual ability, which wants to reveal hidden and embarrassing truths behind the seemingly boundless rainbow of human hypocrisy, even when there may be none. Like his friend-foe Richard Wagner, Nietzsche loved to *épater la bourgeoisie* [shock the bourgeois] and, above all, *les bourgeoises* [the bourgeois ladies].

Secondly, prudential reasons, which I explained in the previous chapter, advise that, when evaluating human actions, we should look *in primis* [first of all] at the most blatant forms of cruelty and that, in order to achieve this goal, we should start always from the victim's perspective. Starting from the perpetrator's perspective could lead us to justify avoidable instances of cruelty as necessary evils. The same prudential reasons lead to the neglect of the drive to distinction as focus-point, because there are minor and major forms of cruelty. The worse forms, involving a severe disproportion in the distribution of power (e.g. the fundamentalist father and his daughter), should be dealt with first. Nietzsche's drive to distinction refers instead to subtler–if not doubtful–cases of cruelty. It is obvious that a group of policemen beating mercilessly a peaceful protester are being cruel. It is less obvious that a chaste nun is being cruel toward the child-bearing mother by being chaste. She, or her inherited subconscious dispositions, might intend to be cruel. The Judeo-Christian God is commonly said to be able to peer into a person's heart, of which she herself may have a muddled grasp. Can Nietzsche really do the same as God?

Moreover, *mens rea*—not to mention some peculiarly Freudian *id reum* [culpable subconscious]—is not enough for cruelty to subsist. Harm must be effectively produced *too*, for, in a mirror-like manner, someone may suffer from the sight of a virtuous person, but the virtuous person's intention may be all but cruel. Finally, cruelty resulting from the drive to distinction implies competition and competition, in turn, implies a limited power imbalance. When the power imbalance is limited, the power to produce actual harm is also limited. The humble person, the great artist, the chaste nun, the successful politician, the good student and the tenured academic achieve distinction after struggling with others, who have enough ability to count as adversaries. Proud persons, tone-deaf people, nymphomaniac porn stars, indifferent citizens, lazy students and illiterate brutes would never count as adversaries. Only the employee terminated by an arrogant boss seems to fit the bill, especially in times when jobs are scarce on the market and labour unions are weak. Briefly presented in the previous chapter, there seems to be some truth behind Adam Smith's notion of cruelty within the economic order.

The History of European Morals

In the previous chapter, I attempted as well to distinguish between a cruelty of intention, or what could be termed "positive" cruelty, and a cruelty of neglect or callousness, which we may call "negative" cruelty. I talked of a cruelty of human agency, which in turn could be divided itself between that which stems from delight in another's suffering, and that which stems from indifference to another's suffering; this suffering being determined either by the action or by the inaction of the perpetrator.

For help in assessing the implications of the delight/indifference distinction, we can turn to a useful passage in Lecky's monumental 1869 *History of European Morals from Augustus to Charlemagne*.[74] Lecky says in the first volume of this work that the key issue *vis-à-vis* cruelty is to do with "realisation", by which he means the capacity of human beings to realise the effects on others of which their cruel delight/indifference is the cause.[75] By focusing on this question of realisation, Lecky manages to turn the cruelty question into one of civilisation, i.e. the ethical education of humankind. "To an uneducated man", Lecky says, "all classes, nations, modes of thought and existence foreign to his own are unrealised, while every increase in knowledge brings with it an increase of insight, and therefore sympathy".[76] But Lecky stipulates that the addition to knowledge is "the smallest part of this change".[77] The most important consideration is the way in which the realising faculty is itself intensified: "Every book he reads, every intellectual exercise in which he engages, accustoms him to rise above the objects immediately present to his senses, to extend his realizations into new spheres, and reproduce in his imagination the thoughts, feelings, and characters of others, with a vividness inconceivable to the savage."[78] As also acknowledged by Hume and his intellectual heirs, civilisation's effect on us is to endow us with "sensitive humanity" and this means that our "realising faculty" has been cultivated and we should therefore "recoil from cruelty" almost instinctively, as it were.

At this point, Lecky takes up the delight/indifference distinction insisted upon in the first chapter. For him it is "an important distinction to draw... Under the name of cruelty are comprised two kinds of vice, altogether different in their causes and in most of their consequences", Lecky says.[79] There is firstly a cruelty that "springs from callousness and brutality", and then there is "the cruelty of vindictiveness".[80] The first kind of cruelty "belongs chiefly to hard, dull, and somewhat lethargic characters" and "appears most frequently in strong and conquering nations and in temperate climates".[81] This kind of cruelty "is due in very great degree to defective realisation".[82] The "strong and conquering nations" are made up of "insensitive" warriors and colonists. The second kind of cruelty is the cruelty of "delight" and it is "usually displayed in oppressed and suffering communities, in passionate natures, and in hot climates".[83] "Great vindictiveness", he says, "is often united with great tenderness, and great callousness with great magnanimity".[84] By the same token "a vindictive nature is rarely magnanimous, and a brutal nature is more rarely tender".[85] Be this as it may, however, Lecky is confident that both forms of cruelty will be "diminished with advancing civilization".[86] Civilization then works on these two kinds of cruelty, albeit "by different forms and in different degrees".[87] The long-term result of this process should be, on the one hand, that "callous cruelty is diminished before the sensitiveness of a cultivated imagination" and, on the other hand, that "vindictive cruelty is diminished by the substitution of a penal system for private revenge".[88]

Lecky is arguing that we in the West should: (1) be less cruel over time because our realizing faculty has been cultivated over the centuries, making us less indifferent to sensitive humanity; and (2) that we should be less vindictive or cruel of intention because the rise of the modern system of penal justice means that we do not have to seek out those who have injured us ourselves and mete out to them a punishment which in our view they deserve. With the rise of the modern State, we can stand back and watch our public agents administer justice on our behalf. We thus lose the habits of vigilantism—thrashing, maiming and killing—and we become less and less capable of inflicting direct harm on others using our own means.

How true to historical experience Lecky's prediction has been is, however, an open question. Indifference to the woes of other human beings is an almost universal human feature in today's world, as remarked in the first chapter. If cruelty is indifference, it was stated, then almost every person on the planet is cruel, and most certainly those of us in the West who have access to certain knowledge about the suffering masses on Earth and go on with our lives in complete obliviousness to the fact of their misery. Otherwise, as it was written in the first chapter, how is it the case that, with twenty-five thousand children dying each day from hunger and hunger-related diseases, the world has not gone mad with compassion in the suffering-with of these vast masses of innocents? In short, has there been any genuine development of Western morality as Lecky foresaw? For Lecky, progress means less cruelty, but there is aplenty going around. In the 19th century, the idea of progress was the unquestioned faith of the educated classes. In the 21st century, we can no longer say the same. The disagreement over the nature of cruelty in contemporary society reflects a disagreement over whether the modern West and its purposes was, on the whole, a sound project to which reasonable and thoughtful people could be dedicated, or whether there was something misconceived and futile in the whole idea of the improvement of humankind from the start. Can we really escape cruelty?

Nietzsche's insights compel us to look at cases of cruelty that may be caused, at least in their genealogical origin, by the drive to distinction. Most importantly, it forces us to be wary of good intentions as an excuse for cruelty, which may hide in all corners of life. And we must be aware, for cruelty ought to be avoided when possible. To the extent that the term "cruelty" is a value-laden term, it regularly connotes moral turpitude. By the very designation of an act as being "cruel", we mean to say that it was evil and unjust. Nevertheless, this regular blameworthiness raises the specular question of whether cruelty is always cruel, or whether it is sometimes kind, which is to say the right thing to do under certain conditions. We are reminded here of Machiavelli's description of Hannibal's "inhuman cruelty" as perfectly complementing "his other virtues", such that, under certain circumstances, cruelty could be a virtue like wisdom or temperance.[90] The Machiavellian orientation to cruelty is to approach it as, in some sense, a 'necessary evil'. But to talk of 'necessary evils' is in a way to indulge in a certain lamenting.

For Nietzsche, on the other hand, such an attitude bespeaks a certain maligning of life. For him, the question of the utility of cruelty is replaced by the psychological inevitability of cruelty as being very close to the heart of life: "Isn't living assessing, preferring, being unfair, being limited, wanting to be different?"[91] Any time the word "cruel" is used as a moral pejorative, whether it is in connection with gratuitous behaviour or grim necessity, the implication is that it should never happen or have to happen. The world should be otherwise than would allow such a thing as cruelty to endure. But for Nietzsche such an attitude is suggestive of a fatigue with life or an incapacity to love the Earth, or even death-wish in that it is tantamount to rejecting the law of gravity because it makes moving and lifting so arduous. For Nietzsche, who echoes in this attitude his intellectual mentor Arthur Schopenhauer (1788–1860), nature is "wasteful beyond measure, indifferent beyond measure, without purpose and consideration, without mercy and fairness, fertile and desolate and uncertain at the same time."[92] And what he calls "nature" is the element within which we humans live and breathe. As part of nature, we ourselves must inevitably share in these qualities or be liable to the accusation of being unnatural, which is to say in some broad sense unhealthy. Nature, for Nietzsche, connotes above all innocence and freedom from self-condemnation; thus, human beings should strive to see all their doings, including the cruel ones, as innocent as earthquakes, hurricanes and tsunamis.

In light of the seemingly paradoxical and even shocking statements of Machiavelli and Nietzsche, even the distinction between 'perpetrator' and 'victim' is to be reconsidered carefully. In a sense, all of us, all human beings, are bound to find ourselves in the role of both the perpetrator and the victim of cruelty at some point in our lives, e.g. today I am suffering from the cruelty of a Gestapo agent, but yesterday I was brutally mean with my wife or kids. Machiavelli and Nietzsche belong to a minority of Western thinkers who, since the *Melian Dialogue* of Thucydides (ca. 460–400 BC), perceives the human being as bent on dominating over her peers whenever she can. In Thucydides' famous text, the victorious Athenians say to the doomed Melians: "Of the gods we believe, and of men we know, that by a necessary law of their nature they rule wherever they can... all we do is to make use of [this law], knowing that you and everybody else, having the same power as we have, would do the same as we do."[93] Moreover, as James Madison (1751–1836) said when writing as Publius in *The Federalist Papers*, human beings are much more disposed "to vex and oppress each other, than to co-operate for the common good."[94]

The main point here I think is that, morally speaking, there is no essential difference between the Lord Chancellor and the stable boy or dairy maid. Operating in the inevitably hierarchical composition of any human society, from the most 'primitive' tribe to the most 'advanced' post-industrial nation, they are all guilty of cruelty to those in a subordinate or weaker position. This is Nietzsche's "Will to Power" as the deepest force in human psychology as well as the inner nature of all life.[95] Not that it cannot be modified or redirected in its force and direction, or that on this day or that the estate manager might give the groomsman the day off or the latter might give the stable boy a candy. The Will to Power, in any case, lurks behind benevolence too.

Also, even along a strict social hierarchy, there may be ways in which the actual power can move upward, i.e. rising from below and striking higher. We do not have to be familiar with a huge swath of novelistic literature or cinematic tradition to know that if the Earl should take a shine to the dairy maid, her charms will play the role of a great equaliser of the power differential between the two. "Form is power", Thomas Hobbes says, "because being a promise of good, it recommendeth men [or women] to the favour of women [or men]".[96] Similarly, the malicious and incessant gossip of ignorant or envious people can hurt deeply the self- and social esteem of innocent individuals, whose actual fault is that of being far superior in moral character, intellectual capacity, physical beauty or artistic ability. This upward-directed cruelty is just one more manifestation, in Hobbes' view, of a deeper drive pervading social relations throughout: "[I]n the first place, I put for a general inclination of all mankind a perpetual and restless desire of power after power, that ceaseth only in death."[97]

It is particularly interesting to ponder upon Madison's insistence on the human tendency "to vex and oppress". Madison saw himself as setting up a more just and more equal society than had been known hitherto, yet he did not expect this tendency to be less in the new society he was constructing. Indeed, he made it the premise of his whole politico-constitutional system. And no one would claim that Madison lacked high expectations for the future and what might be accomplished if society would only become more enlightened and pursue a course of radical reform. In a word, the fact of cruelty or cruel intentions will be operative at some level in any society, no matter how just and democratic it can bring itself to be. If the claims of Madison here, together with those of Machiavelli, Nietzsche, Thucydides and Hobbes, be allowed some weight, then it is strictly speaking impossible to discriminate between victims and perpetrators in an absolute and clear-cut manner. It is not just the 'winners', e.g. the artist, the nun, the politician, the student, the academic, etc. who are the cruel ones, but also the 'losers' e.g. the proud, the nymphomaniac, the lazy-bones, the indifferent, the brutes, and such who are capable and sometimes guilty of radical evil. Their social standing is unequal, perhaps, but there are no saints on this score, only sinners, whether actual or potential. We can recall here the famous line from the second scene in Act 2 of William Shakespeare's (1564–1616) *Hamlet*: "Use every man after his desert, and who should 'scape whipping?"[98]

Perspective 2 – Existentialism

One of the closing remarks from the previous chapter hinted at a provocative hypothesis: existence itself—or otherwise named, nature, life, the universe—can be cruel. It is not only people that can be cruel. Fate can be cruel too, if not crueller—or not? Clearly, detriment of all sorts affects the life of most creatures, if not of all of them, insofar as they experience want, disease, ageing and death. Yet, this detriment is often the result of events that appear to have no intentional agency at work behind them. How can there be cruelty, then? Cruelty seems to entail some degree of moral responsibility which, in turn, entails some form of intentional agency, whether direct or indirect, actively detriment-seeking or wilfully blind. Does existence, nature, life, or the universe, possess any intentional agency?

Goodbye, Cruel World

On the one hand, the answer is most obviously negative. We dwell in a valley of tears: *c'est la vie* [that's life]. The notion of cruelty applied to entities incapable of intentional agency is not appropriate or, at most, merely symbolic. "Not appropriate" implies that we know what the actual, proper understanding of cruelty should be like, though. "Symbolic" does not, for it indicates a mere convergence of opinions or widespread tendency. In effect, the existing literature comprises some cases of just such a linguistic usage, which is not extremely common, or even so common as the one involving intentional agency, especially amongst ethicists. Common sense, though sceptical *prima facie* [at first sight], does not discard entirely such a possibility, insofar as, for instance, the "cruel world" from which the self-murderer escapes is neither entirely nonsensical (who cannot grasp at least some of the reasons for which a person wishes to die?) nor uncommon (around 30,000 people a year commit suicide in the US alone). Hence, let us conclude that such a meaning of "cruelty" is, at least, symbolic.

On the other hand, one may answer affirmatively: there is some form of intentional agency behind the world's imposition of detriment onto the living ones, which we may even want to praise. For instance, we saw in the previous chapter how the Marquis de Sade speaks of cruelty as "nothing but the human energy that civilisation has not yet corrupted... Cruelty, far from being a vice, is the first sentiment that Nature has imprinted within ourselves." Analogous, but with a tragically different twist, is Giacomo Leopardi's description of Nature as "our common mother... an immense female figure, sitting on the ground with her torso erect, leaning on the side of a mountain... with a face partly beautiful and partly frightening, and with the darkest eyes and hair", who cares not for her children.[99] Leopardi writes of an unfortunate Icelander that, while wandering around the world in the vain attempt to find a trouble-free spot where to settle, met accidentally this sublime giantess, who said onto him:

> *Did you believe that the world had been created for you? You must know that in my makings, orders, and operations, and with very few exceptions, I have always had and still have intents that do not contemplate men's happiness or unhappiness. Whenever I offend you in any way or fashion, I don't realise it, if not in very rare cases; and usually, if I please or help you, I don't know it; I didn't do, as you believe, such things or actions to please you or to offer you aid. Indeed, if it happened that I make your entire species extinct, I would not be aware of it.* [100]

Friedrich Nietzsche, possibly recovering Sade's stronger-than-detriment *joie de vivre* [joy of life], commends "cruelty... as one of the oldest and most unrationalizable cultural substrata"[101] and conceives of it as part of nature's "sorry scheme of things", i.e. an endless chain of "begetting, living and murdering".[102] Nietzsche's bleak, characteristically late-19th-century socio-Darwinist understanding of reality influenced many 20th-century thinkers, such as Antonin Artaud (1896–1948), Clément Rosset (b. 1939), and, most importantly, Gilles Deleuze (1925–1995) and Félix Guattari (1930–1992).

Deleuze and Guattari claim that civilisation starts with the institution of the State apparatus—no matter how minimal and barbaric this apparatus may be—which is meant to mould and control its members by all sorts of symbolic means: dialects, taboos, totems, textbooks, mating rituals, penal codes, etc. Fundamentally, any such apparatus relies upon the constriction of biological individuals within the categories of social life, which one achieves initially by inscription of "signs directly on the body... a system of cruelty, a terrible alphabet [of...] blood, torture, and sacrifices."[103] Once this apparatus is firmly established, then can the State function efficiently. Furthermore, the State's need for super-individual standards turns any individual deviance from the governing "system of signs" into the utmost crime, and utilises cruelty in order to keep this danger at bay: "Above all, the State apparatus makes the mutilation, and even death, come first. It needs them preaccomplished, for people to be born that way, crippled and zombielike."[104] Consistently with this picture of social life, the State is said to be an "Anal Oedipus", i.e. an obsessive accumulator of chaos-prone individuals, who hates the father-chaos from whom all were born, back to whom all would naturally lead him, and against whom he forces all to work, i.e. against themselves, by coercing them in all sorts of manners, whether physically or psychologically, everywhere and in every possible moment of their lives.

Somewhat hard to grasp at first, Deleuze's and Guattari's grim picture of the State draws from their direct professional experience in the field of psychotherapy. Their philosophy is pervaded by the awareness of the complex and extensive consequences of the generally unnoticed and, perhaps, tragically (cruelly?) inevitable traumas of the social development of the human psyche, particularly during childhood, when spontaneity and originality are driven out by the adults in favour of conformity and predictability. In their account, like Sade and Leopardi before them, Deleuze and Guattari relate the unavoidable presence of cruelty in the world to some kind of intentional agency. Specifically, Deleuze and Guattari personify the State as the fundamental source of cruelty, thus allowing for the ascription of moral responsibility to an agent, no matter how unique or peculiar this agent may be. By revealing the works of the "Anal Oedipus", they implicitly stress the importance of the notions of moral responsibility and of intentional agency for the possibility itself of conceiving of cruelty.

We could say that the personification of impersonal entities is, again, merely symbolic. By this, however, I do not intend to dismiss the work of Sade, Leopardi, Deleuze and Guttari with a shrug. On the contrary, I regard it as plausible and ethically significant, for it advances from the fear of blurring the distinction between 'actual' cruelty, which points indignantly at the evildoer, and a blame-insensitive cruelty, which 'sprays' evil onto all possible dimensions of being and reduces the space available for any sensible ascription of guilt. Possibly, one can find a solution to the apparent threat of blame-insensitive cruelty by considering that, were existence cruel in itself, then the blameworthy evildoer would be the one who does not care about the amount of detriment deriving from her actions. Such an individual would not try to achieve a certain goal with the least degree of detriment reasonably foreseeable. Instead, she would display indifference to the detriment involved by her action. Indeed, she could also derive delight in producing that detriment, as she opts for measures that cannot but manifestly involve or amplify the detriment. In other words, even if it were impossible not to be cruel, we would still have to decide whether to act under the assumption that we are trying to minimise the detriment to come (i.e. to act morally) or not (i.e. to act immorally), either by being indifferent to the detrimental outcome (i.e. to act brutally) or by maximising it (i.e. to act sadistically).

The Phenomenal Gaze

It is often the case that the phenomenal experience of the truth of a thing—in this case, of cruelty—challenges our conventional notions of truth itself and raises new questions in regard of our fundamental assumptions concerning things. The phenomenal gaze looks upon the lived experience of a subject and attempts to discover and articulate, in its most trusting sincerity, the truth of the subjective encounter of a thing or event, rather than some certain, scientific, objective, trans-personal 'Truth' that exists for all subjects. In regard of the subject's phenomenological understanding of nature, then, the lived experience of nature's event often tells another story from the cold, objective, scientific account that refuses will or intent to the natural world. The scientist may claim that nature is without evil or beneficent intent; nature may will no good or ill consequences to human life. Yet, when we find ourselves confronted with Mother Nature in the raw—whether beset by a lightning storm in the reserve lands of rural Zimbabwe where fiery spears seem to lash out from the angry skies and to stalk the unlucky traveller, or whether teetering at the mouth of Mount Volcano, reeling under the choking breath that menaces from the depths of the Earth—the experience is often one of being targeted by a threatening menace, force or agent, driven by a very personalised objective and acting under an intention of cruelty. Mother Nature can appear to the terrified subject under her thrall as a wickedly malevolent parent with an enormous grudge to bear against me or a cruel indifference to my suffering.

In the work of post-Holocaust phenomenologist Emmanuel Levinas, the elemental is presented in this way—as the realm of faceless, malevolent gods, taunting and menacing the terrified ego, even in the paradox of that ego's at-home-ness and enjoyment of the element. Levinas expresses this paradox as follows:

To be affected by a side of being while its whole depth remains undetermined and comes upon me from nowhere is to be bent toward the insecurity of the morrow. The future of the element as insecurity is lived concretely as the mythical divinity of the element. Faceless gods, impersonal gods to whom one does not speak, mark the nothingness that bounds the egoism of enjoyment in the midst of its familiarity with the element.[105]

Another post-Holocaust phenomenologist, Hans Jonas (1903–1993), sees danger in this view of natural forces. Jonas' naturalist theology seeks to provide ethically motivational counter-metaphors to what he sees as a lineage of nihilistic thought descending from his controversial intellectual father-figure, Martin Heidegger (1889–1976), who was an academic star in Nazi Germany. Jonas diagnoses, in this variety of modern nihilisms, the need to reconfigure the Earth Mother in a more positive light, so he attempts to re-metaphorise her in the tradition of the Greek ancients, as the hallowed ground of a sacred responsibility to preserve life as a good in itself and for its own sake, and not, as transpires under the technological frenzy of modernity, as a good for the sake of something else (e.g. profit, expedience or accumulation of wealth). Since Heidegger's existentialism had uncritically reasserted the metaphysical assumption of a dualism between the human world and nature, nature was reconfirmed as having little value of its own and as being indifferent to human purposes.[106] Thus were lost the divine foundations of the cosmic order; the ancient gods of Thales' (of Miletus, ca. 620-546 BC) pious world-view abandoning the human world to chaos, both metaphysical and moral. As Jonas states:

If values are not beheld in vision as being (like the Good and the Beautiful of Plato), but are posited by the will as projects, then indeed existence is committed to constant futurity with death as its goal; and a merely formal resolution to be, without a nomos [divine law, cultural edict] for that resolution, becomes a project from nothingness to nothingness.[107]

In short, if Heidegger is right about *Dasein's* [i.e. the living and self-reflective person's] meaning-positing here-being, nature does not care. For Jonas, that doctrine is ethically perilous and he asserts: "That nature does not care, one way or the other, is the true abyss."[108] And this conviction composes an abyss that cannot help but culminate in radical nihilism, existentially expressed by its faithful in both a lack of concern for the suffering bodies of the Earth and an impoverished attitude toward life itself articulated in the vapid hyper-consumerist credo: "Let us eat and drink. For tomorrow we must die."[109] Hans Jonas recognises that to remove the intention (good, evil, just, punitive, sacred, benevolent, jealous, etc.) from our understanding of Mother Nature, is to banish the gods from the Earth and, in ethical effect, to relieve us of our responsibilities to the planet and its creatures: "There is no point in caring for what has no sanction behind it in any creative intention."[110] Perhaps one might even see an explanation of Heidegger's flirtation with National Socialism in the nihilistic conclusions implied in his philosophy. If nature has no meaning but the one that the living persons ascribe to her, then the same can happen to entire societies or even persons themselves; if enough people claim Jews, communists and the handicapped to be unworthy of life, then they can be exterminated with equanimity, as the Nazi regime almost succeeded in doing.

The scientists, with Nietzsche, tell us without hesitation that destructive forces are part of the natural power-mix. Coming-to-be entails passing-aways that time dictates as just and as right as the attendant phenomenon of material decay. There is however a certain evil in the human (and animal?) experience of the natural (e.g. ageing and death) that cannot be logically denied, even by the most objective and rationalistic scientist.[111] Philosophers must, with Socrates, remain utterly humble about what certain knowledge we may hold in regard of such mammoth questions. What, ultimately, matters, philosophically and ethically, is not whether Nature is indeed cruel, but whether *we* perceive her to be capable of cruel (and benevolent and punitive and jealous and compassionate) intent. Without the mother in Mother Nature, human beings may not feel called to the accountability of the good child, nor, by extension, to the obligation of the brother's keeper.

Perspective 3 – Bioethics

The cruelty of disease is a sub-topic of the alleged cruelty of existence, nature, life, or the universe, at least insofar as the working definition of cruelty employed here lists general features encompassing the real suffering and the display of either delight in or indifference to it, and accompanying diseases in general. To this condition of actual suffering brought about by an indifferent or delighted agent, the perspective from which the action is being evaluated has to be considered too, hence asking to take into account not only the agent's intentions, but also and even primarily the victim's suffering.

As it was argued in the preceding chapter, prudential reasoning requires that the victim's accusations, rather than the agent's declared aims, be the starting point for the assessment of cruelty. Using this approach to cruelty can explain as well why there are so many references to the cruel character of diseases in the philosophical and literary traditions of the West. To recall just an instance amongst many, in his *Confessions*, Jean-Jacques Rousseau includes disease in a long list of cruelties suffered by him and other human beings. And looking further back in history, Seneca's seventieth letter includes an oft-quoted apology of rational suicide as the ultimate remedy against cruelty:

> *Should I wait for the cruelty of disease or man, when I can leave through the midst of the torments and sweep aside the obstacles. This is one reason why we cannot complain about life: it keeps no one. It is a good thing about human affairs that no one is miserable except by his own fault. If you enjoy life, live. If not, you can return to the place you came from.*[112]

Concerning the interest of such an analysis of the cruelty of disease, I believe it is worth considering because there is something paradoxical yet deeply insightful about the claim that existence, nature, life, or the universe could be cruel. Moral reasoning traditionally distinguishes two types of evil: moral and natural. The standard view is that moral evil is the product of human agency and so includes phenomena such as "war, torture and psychological cruelty", and that natural evil is the product of non-human agency, hence including natural disasters such as "earthquakes, floods, disease and famine".[113] In this standard view, disease is a natural evil, and as such it is the product of an agency to which intentions are not easily attributed.

One, of course, might appeal to the recourse of a God who intends natural evil as a punishment or test for the human species, thus moralising it, but this is a line of thought that I do not pursue here. Instead, my starting assumption is that disease belongs to a more complex set of cases, which are appropriately analysed as a combination of moral and natural evils. The differentiation between disease and non-disease is fundamental to the theoretical and practical performance of medicine and to the life sciences in general, and is consequential to policy, legal and ethical standards in healthcare. Naturalist theories claim that disease is a value-neutral concept to be described by biology. On the other hand, normativist theories argue that the concept of disease is a social convention. With this background in mind, I would like to ask in what ways disease could be meaningfully said to be cruel.

First we should have a look at the existing definitions of disease. After a careful review of the philosophical literature on the subject,[114] Rachel Cooper defines disease as "a condition that it is a bad thing to have, that is such that we consider the afflicted person to have been unlucky, and that can potentially be medically treated".[115] The bad-thing criterion is required to distinguish the biologically different from the diseased, whilst the bad-luck criterion is needed to distinguish diseases from conditions that are unpleasant but normal (Cooper proposes teething as an example). From this definition we can begin to understand why diseases are so often considered as cruelties. If, for an act to be cruel, it must cause suffering (a bad thing) and it must be caused on someone who could reasonably have hoped to have been treated otherwise (i.e. bad luck for him or her), then "cruelty" might well apply in the case of disease. Moreover, if we scrutinise deeper the concept of disease, we can find the same emphasis on perspective that has appeared in the preceding discussion of cruelty.

Refining and improving the World Health Organisation's definition of health as "a state of complete physical, psychological and social wellbeing", Hoffman has described the concept of disease as a triad comprising disease, illness, and sickness.[116] The terms of the triad reflect professional, persona, and social perspectives and concern biological, phenomenological and behavioural phenomena respectively. For him, disease, illness and sickness are negative notions reflecting detrimental occurrences in human life (i.e. bad things) as well as normative notions, because they call for action in the face of bad luck:

> *Disease calls for actions by the medical profession towards identifying and treating the occurrence and caring for the person. Illness changes the actions of the individual, making him or her communicate their personal perspective of the negative occurrence to others, e.g. call for help. Sickness calls for a determination of the social status of the sick person; deciding who is entitled to treatment and economic rights and who is to be exempted from social duties.*[117]

In order to further investigate the cruelty of disease we can then follow three different paths.

Path 1 – *The cruelty of disease from the professional perspective*

In Hoffman's view, disease proper is negative bodily occurrences (i.e. processes, states or events) as conceived of by the medical profession. What kind of cruelty can we find here? Many authors have argued for the essentially culture- and value-laden character of the concept of disease, as well as for the instrumental character of diagnosis, prognosis and treatment. In such accounts, these concepts become warrants for medical interventions enabling the diseased person to improve her condition, but also to suffer invasive or futile procedures that might cause unnecessary pain and suffering. Thus, it is not difficult to read in medical journals controversies including statements such as: "bilateral mastectomy is a cruel intervention which in itself cannot guarantee protection from breast cancer because of residual islands of breast tissue in ectopic sites".[118]

Another controversial issue here is truth-telling. In a clinical context, truth can be cruel, even though this possibility is strongly influenced by cultural and social factors: after a survey of 800 seniors from four different ethnic groups showed that Korean-American and Mexican-American subjects were far less likely than their European-American and African-American counterparts to believe that a patient should be told the truth about the diagnosis and prognosis of a terminal illness, Blackhall and others undertook an ethnographic study to look more deeply at attitudes and experiences of these respondents: they found out that "European-American and African-American respondents were likely to view truth-telling as empowering, enabling the patient to make choices, whilst the Korean-American and Mexican-American respondents were more likely to see the truth-telling as cruel, and even harmful, to the patients".[119]

Path 2 – *The cruelty of illness from the personal perspective*

Illness is negative bodily occurrences as conceived of by the ill person herself.[120] According to Hofmann, the critique of modern medicine directed at its ignorance of the subjective experience of the individual patient, brings about an epistemic and normative primacy of the concept of illness. Although this primacy does not result in an overall subjective approach (because the other two perspectives must be included in the assessment), this coheres with what we stated in the previous chapter on the non-exclusive primacy of the sufferer's perspective. Also, I would like to suggest that illness is felt as cruel not only because the person's pain is caused by an agency that is somehow indifferent to him or her. Diseases are perceived as perfectly arbitrary in their choice of victims, and thus cruel: cancer arbitrarily kills people and thus people are victims of its cruelty. As Susan Sontag (1933–2004) argues in her 1978 book *Illness as Metaphor*, not only we tend to think that disease is to be blamed for the suffering. Very often, we tend to think as well that the disease is the patient's fault, and therefore that the patient herself is to be blamed. This punitive concept of disease might have to do with our own inability to think of disease as a pure instance of natural evil. In order to face it, we look at disease with an anthropomorphic disguise, and thus it becomes an instance of moral evil.

Path 3 – *The cruelty of sickness from the social perspective*

The third concept of the triad, sickness, is negative bodily occurrences as conceived of by the society or its institutions. Here we must remember the early work of Michel Foucault (1926–1984) and its bold challenge to the modern use of the terms "mad" and "mentally ill" as synonyms.[121] Beginning in the 19th century, doctors and other therapists rejected such traditional conceptions of madness as divine ecstasy or diabolical possession in favour of what they believed to be the enlightened view, i.e. that madness is mental illness. The implication of Foucault's analysis for our purposes is that the cruelty of sickness is to be attributed to society itself. After all, there was, even in the relatively recent past of our own culture, a view of madness which was radically different from our own and, as we can infer from Foucault's extensive research, no less defensible. This alone, he suggests, should begin to undermine our idea that there is something inevitable about our conception of madness. The modern experience of madness as mental illness restores a social locus to madness, seeing it as a deviation from norms (a sickness), not a rejection of the entire framework of rationality that defines these norms. He takes particular pains to show that, in spite of its veneer of scientific objectivity, the modern view is based more on a moral disapproval of the values implicit in madness than on any objective scientific truth.

Concluding Remarks

In conclusion, by this discussion of the multi-dimensional cruelty of disease I hope to have shed some light on the different perspectives involved, thus stressing the complexity of ways in which we attribute cruelty to events, processes or states of things, and substantiate further the acknowledgement of the tensions that can arise between the perspectives of the agent and the sufferer of cruelty. I have argued that in the limited scenario of the clinical relationship, we must distinguish among: (1) the perspective of disease, where cruelty lies in the agent's (namely, the medical staff's) evaluation; (2) the perspective of illness, where it lies in the patient's; and, finally, (3) the perspective of sickness, where it lies in an institution or in the society as a whole.

Chapter 3: Two Questions about Liberalism of Fear

Question 1 – *Is Liberalism of Fear Wrong?*

To answer this question, a brief introductory outline of Judith Shklar's (1928–1992) and Richard Rorty's (1931–2007) "liberalism of fear" is needed. Both thinkers claim the fundamental tenet of liberalism to be its staunch opposition to cruelty, which they regard as the least liberal feature of any human community. Of all the nasty things that we can do, it is by far "the worst".[122] This ethical characterisation of liberalism and its associated democratic capitalism has not encountered much opposition. One exception, however, is the self-styled conservative thinker John Kekes (b. 1936), whose critique of liberalism of fear and liberalism at large serves here *qua* starting point for my own critique of the Shklar-Rorty thesis. Additionally, I refer to the Italian Enlightenment penal reformer Cesare Beccaria (1738–1794) and his famous 1764 book *On Crimes and Punishments*, which is deemed to have inspired single-handedly a titanic wave of penal reforms throughout 18th- and 19th-century Europe and Americas.[123] Though a committed reformer and an iconic Enlightenment thinker, Beccaria conceived of cruelty as an integral component to the liberal social order.

The phrase "liberalism of fear" encapsulates a philosophical conception of liberalism *qua* opposition to cruelty, which is judged to be the worst human vice. Cruelty, under this perspective, is the worst thing people are capable of. As to a definition of cruelty, Judith Shklar writes that cruelty is "the wilful inflicting of physical pain on a weaker being in order to cause anguish or fear" and that it "repels instantly because it is ugly" and "disfigures human character".[124] On a similar note, she states: "cruelty is the deliberate infliction of physical, and secondarily emotional, pain upon a weaker person or group by stronger ones in order to achieve some end, tangible or intangible, of the latter."[125] Inasmuch as cruelty feeds upon fear, which inevitably destroys freedom by making people afraid to act as they would want to, cruelty contradicts the central value of the liberal tradition. By strangling individual freedom, cruelty shatters the presuppositions for authentic intersubjective coexistence, in both the public and the private spheres. Therefore, insofar as liberalism wishes to coordinate politically any collective decision-making process, liberalism must be maximally alert to whatever insurgence of cruelty may occur within society. According to liberalism of fear, the pivotal differences between political systems are those related to when, how and why cruelty may be retained or introduced as an instrument for social determination. If, on one extreme, there may be violent military repression, on the other extreme stands a careful system of severely limited public intervention within the lives of citizens, whose security may justify such intervention, in line with traditional liberal principles. The citizens' freedom and security are the two pillars upon which debate can then unfold, making confrontation a peaceful albeit at times unsavoury affair. The latter extreme is, of course, the liberal set-up, which combines all sorts of legal instruments for the sake of keeping cruelty at bay (e.g. an independent judiciary, constitutional protections, human rights). As Shklar writes, these legal, exquisitely liberal instruments "put cruelty first".[126]

Any society where cruelty is abundant is an atomised society, comprising isolated victims and paranoid sadists; it is a society with arbitrary rules that citizens cannot but obey. There is no room for dialogue in it. There is no room for genuine personal self-expression, growth and fulfilment. There cannot be authentic individuality, but only powerless victims, on the one side; whilst on the other side, seemingly omnipotent tyrants spend their lives making sure that their superior standing is not threatened. The cruel State is a frozen State, where political agency is congealed; it is the stable but lifeless rigidity of a corpse. Life is action, though. Instability is then the price that liberals are willing to pay for liberty's sake. In their name are they willing to accept "contradiction, complexity, diversity, and the risks of freedom".[127]

Liberalism of fear has met with very little criticism. Not only does it sound plausible or even desirable; also, who would ever speak well, if not in favour, of cruelty? John Kekes is an exception to the norm. His article "Cruelty and Liberalism" dares launch a critique of the Shklar-Rorty thesis about liberals abhorring cruelty like no one else, as well as of liberalism as such.[128] First of all, Kekes argues that to define liberalism as the rejection of cruelty is a mere "slogan" that cannot withstand the simplest critical scrutiny: is cruelty really "the worst thing we do?"[129] What about "genocide, terrorism, betrayal, exploitation, humiliation, brutalization, tyranny, and so forth?"[130] Liberalism of cruelty is based upon a tautology: all serious evils are seriously evil. Secondly, by suggesting that liberalism's quintessence is its opposition to cruelty, the Shklar-Rorty thesis "insinuates that nonliberals are less opposed to cruelty than liberals and that those who are appropriately outraged by cruelty have willy-nilly joined the ranks of liberals".[131] In Kekes' view, this stance confounds the diversity of possible ethical and political conceptions available: cruelty can be opposed by conservatives too, among others. Additionally, Kekes argues that by granting more freedom to private agency, liberalism expands, rather than reduces, the possibilities for acting cruelly. Given humankind's long-tested propensity to do evil, Kekes claims that liberalism does not prioritise the threat of cruelty, but the maximisation of personal liberty, including its attendant risks, which extend to cruelty.

Unlike the champions of liberalism of fear, Beccaria, a renowned member of the classical liberal canon, offers an internal critique of the same. In his view, cruelty is intertwined with the brighter side of liberalism. Whilst defending the values of liberalism as the path to be followed, Beccaria concedes nonetheless that cruelty can survive, if not even prosper, within the liberal State. His celebrated masterpiece, the book *On Crimes and Punishments*, does not only argue that cruelty is present within a fully reformed, 'modern' judiciary *cum* [inclusive of] penal system, but also and above all in the economic sphere.

Beccaria is a celebrated penal reformer, who embodies the typical Enlightenment virtues of humane tolerance, prudent rationality and moral moderation. Also, he is famous as a utilitarian thinker *ante litteram* [before the term was coined]: penal institutions are deemed good, according to him, if they produce good social outcomes. It is hardly possible to think of a penal system, at least in the West, that was not reformed, at some point, along the lines proposed by Beccaria, especially with regard to the abolition of torture, gruesome corporal chastisements and capital punishment. *Pace* [notwithstanding] the venerated traditions of ecclesiastical and aristocratic justice of his day, Beccaria promotes new conceptions and new methods within the penal sphere, yet he never denies the essentially cruel character of lawful punishment *per se* [as such]. Rather than abolishing cruelty in itself, Beccaria's reformism aimed at doing away with unnecessary and irrational cruelties in the penal institutions of Europe and, indirectly, their colonial possessions across the world. As he writes, "punishments" are "atrocious" and their "public and solemn cruelty" can only be lessened by making them "useful... necessary... fair" and consistent with "the goal of the laws".[132] A lesser and perhaps necessary evil, penal cruelties remain cruel though rationally administered, proportional to the severity of the crimes committed and, above all, sensibly directed to the betterment of the society in which the penal institutions operate.

As to any liberal society, there is an additional level at which cruelty persists, often unseen. Beccaria, in fact, argues that the crime of "theft" is nothing but the result of an institution, without which no liberal society could exist: "private property".[133] By allowing people to own things privately and seek, *via* commercial activity, an even bigger share of the things that can be owned privately, this commonplace institution causes great disparities in wealth to emerge within society. In close association with these great disparities, there emerge too the "misery and despair" of multitudes who must endure "nothing but a bare existence": it is precisely from the ranks of such paupers that those guilty of "theft" typically arise, as they try to improve their lot by stealing to those who own significant property, or any.[134] Theft being a crime that requires lawful punishment for its restraint and correction, the cruelty of property leads to the cruelty of judicially sanctioned chastisements. It is a sorry and almost paradoxical state of affairs; but it is one for which Beccaria sees no alternative.

Question 2 – *Is Liberalism of Fear Right?*

Kekes and Beccaria, despite their very different background, offer some serious food for thought. Could it be that, despite Shklar's and Rorty's protestations, cruelty is part and parcel of liberalism, and that its thorough avoidance is not, *a fortiori*, the defining characteristic of the liberal tradition? On the one hand, Kekes tells us that liberals, by enlarging the scope of individual free agency, make effectively more room for cruelty, since cruelty is an option for any free agent. Beccaria, on the other hand, goes even deeper in his critique, for he sees cruelty as ingrained within basic liberal institutions, i.e. penal justice and private property, and claims that the latter, by generating misery, also generates crime, which in turn is punished *via* the former and then, such punishments being inherently cruel, there is no way left to avoid cruelty. Are they correct in their criticisms? Or is there anything amiss?

One way to meet Kekes' critique is to notice how it actually explains why liberals entertain an ironic relationship with cruelty: they reject it but cannot get rid of it. They do know that liberty can foster cruelty, but they are unwilling to sacrifice liberty *qua* political ideal, whilst at the same time keeping in mind that cruelty is indeed the worst that we can do and that, therefore, they must be indefatigably vigilant, whether in the public or in the private sphere. Back in the 19th century, a motto known to the US citizens was: "the price of liberty is eternal vigilance".[135] On his part, in *Contingency, Irony, and Solidarity*, Rorty gives prime importance to writers such as George Orwell (1903–1950) and Vladimir Nabokov (1899–1977), i.e. discoverers of forms of cruelty that, until their time, had not been fully grasped. They made the invisible visible. As to the cruelty intrinsic to the penal system, it may be true that it cannot be avoided and that liberalism, by not renouncing the penal system, endorses it. Still, which ideological or political system can do without it? If it is cruel because endowed with a penal system, then liberalism is as cruel as socialism, conservatism or Christian democracy. The issue of cruelty is certainly an issue for the law. Yet are crimes and punishments essentially cruel, as Beccaria argues? Can there be a punishment that is not cruel?

According to Páll Árdal (1924–2003), Icelandic philosopher and historian of philosophy, the issue of "ill desert" arises whenever choosing the penultimate evil that another must endure for the sake of some ultimate good, e.g. when a parent strives to determine the appropriate punishment for a naughty child, whose moral education the parent has at heart.[136] When chastising young Johnny for pulling his sister's hair, the parent is trying to let Johnny understand that he must not do it, for his action, i.e. pulling her hair, harms his sister. If needed, the parent ought to pull young Johnny's hair to make him realise it. The ultimate objective of this seemingly cruel intermediate action is to improve Johnny's understanding of other human beings by means of sympathetic imagination. The hope is that Johnny will eventually feel pain at the sole prospect of harming another. If his temporary pain means furthering little Johnny's ability to sympathise and thus averting future cruelty and injustice, then it is a pain that is sensibly inflicted. Pain can be morally justified when it accompanies virtue, which is not the same thing as inflicting pain simply because someone misbehaved. Unaccompanied by adequate growth in understanding, devoid of development in sympathetic imagination, punishments can actually harden a person's heart and further insensitivity, as Montesquieu had already stated in the 18th century with respect to Japanese society. Incidentally, the hardening of people's hearts and the furthering of insensitivity are the reasons why Beccaria himself opposes the death penalty. Commonly applied throughout Europe, for minor crimes too, the capital punishment's potential for deterrence was minimal while harder and harder punishments ensued, following the same logic, yet possibly as ineffective as the initial one.

Árdal followed in his studies the lead of David Hume, who is renowned for having investigated the importance of emotions in our ethical life.[137] Though sometimes debatable or hazy, Árdal agrees with Hume's overall project and, especially, on the notion that the more morally mature a person is, the more likely she is to suffer when thinking about the injustices and the cruelties of others.

Besides, Hume's philosophy can also teach us about the importance of human imagination within this moral and institutional context. First of all, Hume observes how the imagination affects powerfully all human apprehensions of reality. Secondly, human imagination is said to be more sensitive to the particular than to the general: it is difficult to experience strong feelings, if any at all, if the object of our passion is not well-determined. Thirdly, our passions and the imagination itself are affected by the degree of strength and vivid character of our beliefs, independently of the real existence or non-existence of their supposed objects. Cruelty, as also Beccaria acknowledges, is a by-product of the fear that we experience, which results in turn from the imagination's apprehension of an evil that may or may not exist in reality. In this respect, Kekes and Beccaria do teach us a lesson *vis-à-vis* the liberalism of fear championed by Shklar and Rorty: when cruelty is cast vividly within our imagination, the resulting fear can reinforce another cruelty.

For instance, the 9/11 terrorist attack was certainly cruel, but the fear it ignited in the West engendered the equally cruel, if not crueller retribution by the US and, to a lesser extent, by other countries. This retributive cruelty resorted to warfare on a scale that the world had not seen for generations and that has been producing the collapse and prolonged agony of entire nations in its wake, as well as the increased likelihood of novel terrorist acts. Whenever fear leads to more of the same as the sole possible reply, cruelty blocks the blossoming of sympathetic imagination.

Yet, cruelty is more than the mere freezing paralysis or blockage of morally decisive sensibility. Cruelty cannot be reduced to the absence of a positive. Nietzsche himself had already observed that cruelty, unlike brutality, shares with sympathy the ability to perceive another's suffering. The cruel person needs to know that she is causing pain. The imagination at fault in the cruel person is not the one required to imagine pain, but the one needed to put oneself into another's place, i.e. sympathetic imagination, whereby one makes well-rounded emotional sense of another's discomfort and can identify emotionally with her. It is the imagination of the novelist who, for a while, can transform herself into another person and transmit that person's experiences to the reader. This is how Ian McEwan (b. 1948), for example, understands the literary phenomenon: novels do not exist for the sake of telling people how to live, but rather to exhibit how different lives are lived. This kind of imagination is the foundation of all "sympathy, empathy and compassion", according to him, and cruelty develops from the malfunctioning of this power.[138]

There is then a plausible way out for the Shklar-Rorty thesis, namely the recognition of the ironic relationship that liberals entertain with cruelty, insofar as they will never be able to get rid of it completely, but can and ought to be vigilant in order to minimise its disruptive effects. If and when liberalism of fear dares more and claims that cruelty must be put first, however, as though the other central values of liberalism could be derived from the institutional impairment of cruelty, then serious theoretical problems arise. Whenever freedom is at risk, then the liberal anti-cruelty stance loses its primacy. Shklar and Rorty, in brief, would better describe their liberalism in a far more traditional fashion, namely by reference to the primacy of freedom. Cruelty, when it is not opposed to freedom, finds far too easily decent enough clothes to wear in public. They may be the clothes of just retaliation, penal justice and education, for example, or those of competitive entrepreneurship, marketability of skills and trickle-down economics, whereby present pains and concrete personal tragedies are accepted in the name of prospected long-term wealth creation. In any case, cruelty survives therein. Of course, its survival might be a mere externality, an unintended effect, common to other ideologies and political set-ups. Still, if this externality is caused by liberalism too, as Kekes' reflections and Beccaria's critique entail, then it is not inappropriate to conclude that cruelty is actively brought into being and kept alive by liberalism. Whether many liberals would accept this conclusion as an unavoidable limitation of their political doctrine is contentious. Necessary evil may be tragically inevitable, at times, or even all the time. Liberalism may still be the best option on the table, despite its cruelty and pain—warts and all.

PART II – Cruelty in the History of Thought

Chapter 4: No Pain, No Gain. The Understanding of Cruelty in Western Philosophy

We read in the previous chapter that Richard Rorty claims that "liberals are the people who think that cruelty is the worst thing we do",[139] joining *ipso dicto* [by way of the statement itself] the ranks of the proponents of that liberalism of fear which Judith Shklar started establishing as a recognised liberal strand since the early 1980s. We read also that this strand of liberalism individuates an ultimate dichotomy between force and dialogue, or "between cruel military and moral repression and violence, and a self-restraining tolerance that fences in the powerful to protect the freedom and safety of every citizen."[140] Such a clear-cut opposition to cruelty is taken to connote liberalism in the public sphere, whilst none is as starkly presupposed in the private sphere. In the latter context, Rorty believes the main aim to be "private perfection", or aesthetic "self-creation", not cruel-free "justice" or "human solidarity", as in the public sphere.[141] Rorty goes as far as to affirm that these two aims, i.e. private perfection and solidarity, cannot be reconciled "in a single vision".[142] According to him, "there is no synthesis of ecstasy and kindness", though we may commendably strive for one.[143] Tensions, inconsistencies and contingency cannot be overcome completely.

True to his disavowal of any philosophical foundationalism, i.e. the metaphysical justification of ethics and/or politics, Rorty states as well:

There is no answer to the question "Why not be cruel?" – no noncircular theoretical backup for the belief that cruelty is horrible. Nor is there an answer to the question "How do you decide when to struggle against injustice and when to devote yourself to private projects of self-creation?"... Anybody who thinks that there are well-grounded theoretical answers to this sort of question – algorithms for resolving moral dilemmas of this sort – is still, in his heart, a theologian or a metaphysician... [And a] postmetaphysical culture seems to me no more impossible than a postreligious one, and equally desirable.[144]

Rorty offers no advocacy for private cruelty. Rather, he works out the consequences of Freud's realisation "that in fact everything to do with our life is chance."[145] It is in this way that Rorty's reading becomes open to the possibility that cruelty may colour, if not even at times inform, our private transactions. For instance, ordinary cruelties take place in the education of children, or in the children's persistent and wilful challenges to their parents' better judgment, as well as in the process of separation between parents and children; not to mention the ritual humiliations, the sleepless nights, the heart-breaking crises, and the embarrassing sexual self-discoveries involved in love relationships. Which infatuation, affair, divorce, or lasting marriage has not been affected by some kind of grinding mercilessness by one partner upon the other? Even the decorous and demure Baruch Spinoza (1632–1677) admits that "cruelty is what we do to those we love".[146]

Connoting Cruelty

Perhaps, this use of "cruelty" is equivocal. Parental conundrums and love affairs are not as cruel as, say, police abuse and military action; perhaps they should be treated as different forms of evil. Yet, sticking to a catholic use of "cruelty" would not be entirely arbitrary, for an incredible variety of interpretations and examples of "cruelty" have been offered in the long history of Western thought, many of which are to be summarised hereby in greater detail than in the opening chapter of this book. Out of this *mare magnum* [vast sea] of hypotheses and examples, only diverse and broad criteria can be extracted, focussing on the most frequent connotations of cruelty, e.g.:

1. *Pain*: Whether only physical or also psychological, serious or minimal, justified or unjustified, cruelty implies pain.[147]

2. *Excess*: Whether of pain as such or of its usages to acceptable ends (e.g. penal sanctions), or of our hopes in a tolerable life, or of our abilities to understand reality, cruelty eventually steps 'beyond'—acceptability, tolerability, comprehensibility, sanity, etc.

3. *Roles*: Whether directly or indirectly established, cruelty requires the roles of victim and perpetrator, even when the latter is institutional, impersonal or unknown. In such a two-party relationship, God Himself has been accused of being cruel, as with Job's lamentation in the Old Testament: "You have become cruel to me; with the might of Your hand You persecute me".[148]

4. *Power*: It is only by means of power differential that the roles of victim and perpetrator can be established. Equality stands in cruelty's way. Unequal hierarchies, as discussed in the third chapter, do the opposite.

5. *Mens rea*: Whether delighted in or indifferent to the pain inflicted, the perpetrator possesses a culpable mental attitude. Consistently with this realisation, as we saw in the second chapter, when tackling impersonal and institutional perpetrators, several thinkers have proceeded to personify the universe, nature or the State.

6. *Evil*: Cruelty is a species of evil. Even when conceived of as good, it is either an instrumental evil or an apparent evil, the goodness of which must be revealed and justified, as already exemplified in chapter 1 by Machiavelli's perplexing moral immorality, which is admitted only for the prince who must rule over a community, or the evolutionary benefits in Nietzsche's account of cruelty as drive to distinction.

7. *Paradox*: As noted in the preface, cruelty horrifies and, at the same time, fascinates. This is just one of the many contradictions contained within cruelty, which can be aptly described as paradoxical. The array of diverse conceptions collected below further substantiates this point, and Philip P. Hallie's (1922–1994) philosophy above all.

As diverse, broad and perfectible as they may be, these criteria can assist the reader in perceiving the family resemblances across five recurrent and/or significant conceptions of cruelty, which follow below.

Cruelty as Vice

Cruelty has been regarded very often as a quintessentially human vice affecting specific individuals. This conception of cruelty is characteristic of ancient and medieval philosophers, whose approach to ethics typically centres upon the notion of personal character rather than upon the notion of rightful or good actions and norms— the latter being predominant amongst modern and contemporary thinkers. Also, this former conception of cruelty takes a chief interest in observing what consequences cruelty has for the perpetrator, rather than for its victims, as commonplace instead for modern and contemporary approaches to cruelty. In particular, ancient and medieval philosophers suggested that cruelty is a vice affecting persons involved in punitive contexts, e.g. courtrooms, schools, armies and households.

In *De Clementia*, Seneca claims that "cruel are those who have a reason for punishing, but do not have moderation in it".[149] Besides, as anticipated in the first chapter of this book, he claims that, as concerns the person who "finds pleasure in torture, we may say is not cruelty, but savagery – we may even call it madness; for there are various kinds of madness, and none is more unmistakable than that which reaches the point of murdering and mutilating men."[150] "Cruelty" is thus defined as "harshness of mind in exacting punishment", rather than unrestrained lust for blood.[151] As a vice, "cruelty" is said to be "an evil thing befitting least of all a man",[152] and it can take private forms (e.g. family feuds) as well as public forms (e.g. tyranny, insofar as "[t]yrants", unlike kings resorting to cruelty "for a reason and by necessity[,...] take delight in cruelty").[153] Cruelty is the opposite of clemency, yet "it is as much a cruelty to pardon all as to pardon none."[154] Clemency, according to

Seneca, does not mean indiscriminate forgiveness, but rather a balanced blend of moderation and justice.

As famously discussed by Aristotle, our vices are said to spring from a lack of balance within the human soul; to exceed in forgiveness is as conducive to vice as to exceed in harshness. Aquinas' *Summa Theologica* echoes Seneca's position and combines it with Aristotle's ethics:

> *Cruelty apparently takes its name from "cruditas" [rawness]. Now just as things when cooked and prepared are wont to have an agreeable and sweet savour, so when raw they have a disagreeable and bitter taste. Now it has been stated... that clemency denotes a certain smoothness or sweetness of soul, whereby one is inclined to mitigate punishment. Hence cruelty is directly opposed to clemency.* [155]

Also for the *doctor angelicus* [angelic doctor] of the Catholic Church is "cruelty... hardness of the heart in exacting punishment",[156] hence a form of "human wickedness"; whereas "savagery and brutality" are a form of "bestiality".[157] Cruelty contains an element of rational deliberation, which "savagery" and "brutality" do not possess: these, in fact, "take their names from a likeness to wild beasts... deriving pleasure from a man's torture."[158] Cruelty is therefore something evil that we do intentionally and which corrupts our character by exceeding in what would be otherwise acceptable; but it is also something that we can do something else about, for all vices can be remedied by proper self-correction. As Aristotle and the medieval pedagogues used to teach, whatever the initial endowment of inclinations and talents in our character, each of us is responsible for the kind of person she becomes.

Cruelty as Sadism

The distinction drawn by Seneca and Aquinas between cruelty and bestiality, epitomised by sadistic pleasure, seems to vanish with several modern thinkers, who actually take *sadism* as the paramount, if not the sole, example of cruelty. This is a second, fairly common conception of cruelty, according to which cruelty turns into something worse than a vice, indeed something devilish or extreme. To some, cruelty becomes so extreme a tendency that it transforms into a sheer figment of our imagination, i.e. some kind of philosophical or literary 'ghost'. Thomas Hobbes, for instance, argues that "Contempt, or little sense of the calamity of others, is that which men call cruelty; proceeding from security of their own fortune. For, that any man should take pleasure in other men's great harms, without other end of his own, I do not conceive it possible."[159] Bishop Joseph Butler, on his part, states that "[t]he utmost possible depravity, which we can in imagination conceive, is that of disinterested cruelty."[160] David Hume, on this point, affirms: "Absolute, unprovoked, disinterested malice has never, perhaps, had place in any human breast".[161]

The element of rational deliberation that Seneca and Aquinas observed in cruelty is adamantly underplayed in this second conception of cruelty, as Thomas Hobbes' understanding reveals once more:

> *Revenge without respect to the example and profit to come is a triumph, or glorying in the hurt of another, tending to no end (for the end is always somewhat to come); and glorying to no end is vain-glory, and contrary to reason; and to hurt without reason tendeth to the introduction of war, which is against the law of nature, and is commonly styled by the name of cruelty.*[162]

Rather than a vice, for which a person must take responsibility, cruelty morphs into a malady of the soul, the result of a poor, incompetent or broken mind, which reduces the humanity of its carrier and makes her closer to wild animals. Perhaps, this malady can be cured, or at least confined by appropriate measures of social hygiene. After all, animals can be tamed and trained; though sometimes they are put in cages or butchered. And the cruel human person, now likened to the beast, can be treated instrumentally, like commonly practised with horses and pigs; all this, naturally, being the case for the greater good of the commonwealth to which she and her victims belong.

Cruelty as Harm to Be Avoided

The idea of cruelty as something sick, if not even something sickening, colours also the work of the French Renaissance sceptic Michel de Montaigne, whom the reader encountered in the first chapter. In his *Essays*, Montaigne observes that "cowardice is the mother of cruelty"[163] and states:

> *I cruelly hate cruelty, both by nature and by judgment, as the extreme of all vices. But this is to such a point of softness that I do not see a chicken's neck wrung without distress, and I cannot bear to hear the scream of a hare in the teeth of my dogs... Even the executions of the law, however reasonable that may be, I cannot witness with a steady gaze.*[164]

As for wars, it is worth repeating that Montaigne remarks: "I could hardly be convinced, until I saw it, that there were souls so monstrous that they would commit murder for the mere pleasure of it... For that is the uttermost point that cruelty can attain."[165] The conceptions of cruelty as vice and sadism are accounted for in Montaigne's reflections, but they are also subtly advanced to a broader condemnation of cruelty as harm to be avoided: capital punishment might be reformed, hunting abandoned, and wars prevented. In this perspective, his contribution to the understanding of cruelty in Western history is momentous, just as momentous were his *Essays* for the West's intellectuals in the three centuries following their publication, and it connects the modern conceptions with the ancient one. Moreover, Montaigne is the first Western intellectual to devote an entire essay to the topic of cruelty—a stark sign of how genuine was his hatred for cruelty. "Montaignesque" is therefore the third conception of cruelty to be presented, i.e. cruelty as harm to be avoided.

The champions of the European Enlightenment are probably the most vocal and best-remembered members of this approach. Montesquieu, for example, labels as "cruel... torture" and gruesome "punishments", legal servitude for insolvent debtors, and colonial occupation.[166] In his essays *On Tolerance*, Voltaire (1694–1778) describes as eminently cruel all wars of religion, whilst in *Candide* he condemns as such rape, corporal punishment and mutilation, even when lawfully administered in the name of justice.[167] Adam Smith, champion of the Scottish Enlightenment, ascribes the attribute "cruel" to infanticide,[168] personal *vendetta*,[169] economic monopolies,[170] burdensome taxes of succession or of passage of property,[171] the suffering of the "race of labourers" in periods of economic recession,[172] and mercy to the guilty.[173] In Italy, Pietro Verri (1728–1797) argues that "[r]eason can show [what] is unjust, extremely dangerous, and immensely cruel"—and reason led him to condemn "torture" as "cruel".[174] Cesare Beccaria, the most influential penal reformer of all times and both a friend and a student of Verri's, condemns torture as cruel too, whilst also noting: "man is only cruel in proportion to his interest to be so, to his hatred or to his fear."[175] Hence, it ought to be a duty for the legislator to "[c]ause men to fear the laws and the laws alone. Salutary is the fear of the law, but fatal and fertile in crime is the fear of one man of another. Men as slaves are more sensual, more immoral, more cruel than free men".[176] For Jean-Antoine-Nicolas, Marquis de Condorcet (1743–1794), instead, "cruel" is the institutional neglect of "the progress of education", for it constitutes nothing but the shameful misdeed of "abandoning men to the authority of ignorance, which is always unjust and cruel".[177] Even the non-consequentialist Enlightenment thinker *par excellence*, Immanuel Kant (1724–1804), does espouse the spirit of reformation of his age, and calls "most cruel" the institution of "slavery" exercised in the "Sugar Islands" by Dutch landowners,[178] whereas merely "cruel" are the "duels" fought in the name of "military honour", which, like "Maternal Infanticide", lead to cases of "Homicide" as distinguished from "Murder".[179]

19th- and 20th-century political and legal reformers followed in the footsteps of the 'enlighteners' of the 18th century. Amongst them are also Judith Shklar and Richard Rorty. As we saw in the previous chapter, Judith Shklar, who was a Montaigne scholar, defines cruelty in two ways. The former reads: "Cruelty is... the wilful inflicting of physical pain on a weaker being in order to cause anguish and fear... [it is] horrible... [it] repels instantly because it is 'ugly'... and disfigures human character"[180]. The latter reads: "Cruelty is the deliberate infliction of physical, and secondarily emotional, pain upon a weaker person or group by stronger ones in order to achieve some end, tangible or intangible, of the latter."[181] Judith Shklar believes that cruelty, to a meaningful extent, can be controlled by appropriate doses of liberalism, which is itself in many ways a child of the 18th century: "the first right is to be protected against the fear of cruelty. People have rights as a shield against this greatest of human vices. This is the evil, the threat to be avoided at all costs. Justice itself is only a web of legal arrangements required to keep cruelty in check."[182] Good laws and good political arrangements can reduce the pain that we impose upon/suffer from weaker/stronger creatures like us. That is the hope animating the American and the French Revolutions, as well as many of the emancipatory struggles fought during the following two centuries.

Still, additional cruelties can be retrieved—and rejected—in other areas too. Giacomo Leopardi, for one, aims at a different target. As we read in the first chapter of this book, he associates cruelty with the rewards and punishments awaiting us *post mortem* [after death], which he claims to be nothing but the sorrowful fictional creations of tragically misguided philosophies and religions. Whether "healthy or sick", these creations are, in his view, signs of "cowardice" and mere "childish illusions" that were developed in the face of "the absence of any hope, ...the desert of life, ...men's infelicity[,]... and destiny's cruelty".[183] Though living as such is cruel in and for itself, even crueller it is to live in fear of the priest's gloomy superstitions or the philosopher's hollow concepts.

Tom Regan (b. 1938) sketches a fascinating taxonomy of cruelty, which he derives from yet another area that seems engulfed with cruelty: the human treatment of animals. As Regan writes:

People can rightly be judged cruel either for what they do or for what they fail to do, and either for what they feel or for what they fail to feel. The central case of cruelty appears to be the case where, in Locke's apt phrase, one takes 'a seeming kind of Pleasure' in causing another to suffer. Sadistic torturers provide perhaps the clearest example of cruelty in this sense: they are cruel not just because they cause suffering (so do dentists and doctors, for example) but because they enjoy doing so. Let us term this sadistic cruelty... Not all cruel people are cruel in this sense. Some cruel people do not feel pleasure in making others suffer. Indeed they seem not to feel anything. Their cruelty is manifested by a lack of what is judged appropriate feeling, as pity or mercy, for the plight of the individual whose suffering they cause, rather than pleasure in causing it... The sense of cruelty that involves indifference to, rather than enjoyment of, suffering caused to others we shall call brutal cruelty...Cruelty admits of at least four possible classifications: (1) active sadistic cruelty; (2) passive sadistic cruelty; (3) active brutal cruelty; (4) passive brutal cruelty.[184]

Whichever class of cruelty we encounter in life, Regan believes that we must try to eliminate it. In particular, he focuses on (3) and (4), i.e. the types of cruelty that seem to characterise the human-animal relationship in contemporary societies. Persons are not only cruel to other persons: as long as pain is taken to be a relevant ethical factor, then also animals can become victims, and maybe even perpetrators (though Regan does not explore this avenue).

Cruelty as Paradox

As inheritors of the projects initiated in the 18th century, we can find Shklar's and Regan's definitions rather appealing. However, how many types of cruelty and cruel areas of behaviour can be actually tackled? How many revolutions, with their load of gunpowder and dynamite, should be fought? If three centuries of worldwide-expanding liberalism, culminated with Francis Fukuyama's (b. 1952) post-Cold-War proclamation of "the end of history", have not eliminated it, what reasonable expectations can be entertained *vis-à-vis* the future?[185]

Few are the philosophers who have pondered upon the *paradoxical* character of cruelty—a fourth conception that can also be retrieved in the history of Western thought. Cruelty persists within our lives and societies despite its being commonly denounced as something extremely negative and, above all, despite the recurring attempts to promote social progress and reform existing institutions. Judith Shklar herself admits that "cruelty is baffling because we can live neither with nor without it" and this is probably the reason why:

> *Philosophers rarely talk about cruelty... I suspect that we talk around cruelty because we do not want to talk about it... What we do seem to talk about incessantly is hypocrisy, and not because it hides cowardice, cruelty, or other horrors, but because failures of honesty and of sincerity upset us enormously, and they are vices which we can attack directly and easily. They are easier to bear, and seem less intractable.*[186]

Philip P. Hallie marks a notable exception to the commonplace avoidance of the subject denounced by Judith Shklar. Firstly, Hallie defines "cruelty" as "the infliction of ruin, whatever the motives"[187] or, in two alternative versions, "the activity of hurting sentient beings"[188] and "the slow crushing and grinding of a human being by other human beings".[189] He then distinguishes the instances of "cruelty upon humans" between those "fatal cruelties" that are due to nature and the far from uncommon "human violent cruelty" that is due to our fellow human beings.[190] To the latter he adds "implicit" or "indirect" cruelties, i.e. cruelties arising from "indifference or distraction" rather than from evident "intention to hurt".[191] Thus understood, human cruelty can be further divided into "sadistic" and "practical": whereas the latter refers to forms of instrumental cruelty, the former is "self-gratifying".[192] By way of this articulate taxonomy, richer than Tom Regan's itself, Hallie attempts to encompass and map the vast, polymorphous universe of cruelty, whose intricate nature explains perhaps its little permeability to philosophical analysis. Secondly, Hallie cuts the Gordian knot of cruelty's intrinsic complexity by referring to it as a *paradox*, candidly and straightforwardly—in a book's very title. Why simplifying something that cannot be simplified? Why misrepresenting it, in the attempt to represent it clearly? Hallie has in mind five particular cases of paradoxical cruelty:

1. Cruelty brought about without any open "intention to hurt", but in the name of altruism, happiness, justice, etc.[193] "Substantial maiming" can derive from "wanting the best and doing the worst".[194]

2. Cruelty caused by genuine "intention to hurt", but aimed at educating and therefore avoiding worse cruelties, e.g. "*in terrorem*" [terrifying] literary techniques.[195] As French literary scholar André Dinar (1883–1962) also observes: "The cruel authors cauterise the wounds that can be healed and mark with hot irons the incurable ones, so to expose their horror".[196]

3. "The *fascinosum* [lure] of cruelty",[197] as well as its ability to titillate "sexual pleasure",[198] higher "awareness",[199] the liberation of sensual "imagination"[200] and "masochistic pleasure",[201] are all pursued willingly and proactively, very often, by fully conscious persons.

4. Cruelty implied by the "growth" or maturing of any individual through painful "individualisation" for the sake of "human authenticity".[202] No person becomes mature, well-rounded and responsible without facing a significant amount and variety of

pain in her life, and without learning how to face probable, if not inevitable, later doses of the same bitter medicine.

5. "Responsive" cruelty enacted in retaliation to "provocative" cruelty,[203] e.g. penal chastisements and just wars, although "mitigation" is recommended.[204]

Being a devout Christian, Hallie has no desire to promote cruelty. Quite the contrary, his work on this topic begins as an effort to reduce it. Nevertheless, as he deepens his understanding of it, Hallie comes to recognise that not all cruelty ought to be avoided, for its disappearance would be more harmful than its persistence. This is particularly true of the painful processes of growth and maturation, as well as of artistic disclosure of sorrowful truths or extreme sexual elation. Moreover, in an implicit reminder of Beccaria's own wisdom, Hallie admits that cruelty may be a necessary evil in the public sphere. As baffling as this may be, cruelty seems to find rather easily assorted justifications for enduring in many aspects of life.

Cruelty as Good

Some philosophers have stepped beyond the sole acknowledgment of cruelty's paradoxical character and entertained plainly the seemingly contradictory notion that it might be good. This is the fifth and last conception of cruelty, which comprises two main groups of thinkers.

Instrumentally

In the first group are included those thinkers who have argued that cruelty does not need to have intrinsic value (or disvalue), but instrumental value alone and, as such, that cruelty may be capable of fulfilling a positive function. For instance, cruelty can be a tool to promote the common good. Niccolò Machiavelli, as seen in the first chapter, is among them. According to him:

Every prince ought to desire to be considered clement and not cruel. Nevertheless he ought to take care not to misuse this clemency. Cesare Borgia was considered cruel; notwithstanding, his cruelty reconciled the Romagna, unified it, and restored it to peace and loyalty. And if this be rightly considered, he will be seen to have been much more merciful than the Florentine people, who, to avoid a reputation for cruelty, permitted Pistoia to be destroyed [by the rioting between the Cancellieri and Panciatichi factions in 1502 and 1503].[205]*

Jacques Derrida (1930–2004) states something analogous when he writes: "Politics can only domesticate [cruelty], differ and defer it, learn to negotiate, compromise indirectly but without illusion with it… the cruelty drive is irreducible."[206] Instead of combating cruelty at all costs, one ought to learn how to draw as much good as possible from it. After all, the initiation of social life makes itself use of cruelty: why should its continuation be devoid of it? This is what Gilles Deleuze and Félix Guattari seem to suggest, for example. The acquisition and continuation of the shared semiotic abilities that allow for human communities to develop is never devoid of cruelty. Schooling and socialisation are no free meal: "Cruelty is the movement of culture that is realized in bodies and inscribed on them, belabouring them."[207]

Sharing a similar awareness, Clément Rosset explores the instrumental role of cruelty in the private sphere, rather than the public one, and writes provokingly: "Joy is necessarily cruel".[208] According to him, "[c]ruelty is not… pleasure in cultivating suffering but… a refusal of complacency toward an object, whatever it may be."[209] Now, "the 'cruelty' of the real… is the intrinsically painful and tragic nature of reality."[210] For instance:

[T]he cruelty of love (like that of reality) resides in the paradox or the contradiction which consists in loving without loving, affirming as lasting that which is ephemeral – paradox of which the most rudimentary vision would be to

say that something simultaneously exists and does not exist.
The essence of love is to claim to love forever but in reality to
love only for a time. So the truth of love does not correspond
to the experience of love.[211]

For Rosset, the answer to cruelty's paradox lays in the nature of reality, which is ultimately cruel. Rosset's thought could then be regarded as belonging legitimately to the fourth conception of cruelty as well, i.e. cruelty as paradox. In truth, the distinction between the fourth and the fifth conceptions is not clear-cut, and the same can be said of the distinctions between the other conceptions previously presented (especially between the first and the third, and the second and the third). These distinctions are mostly a matter of different conceptual emphasis, rather than of mutual incompatibility; and as we emphasise the fifth conception, it can be stated that, to a relevant extent, persons are shaped by cruelty and are bound to encounter it also and above all if they wish to derive a modicum of satisfaction from their mortal existence. The only way to live well, for Rosset, who was a Schopenhauer scholar, involves learning to embrace the suffering that life unavoidably unloads upon us.

In the field of drama, Antonin Artaud echoes and expands Rosset's tragic awareness: "Death is cruelty, resurrection is cruelty, transfiguration is cruelty… Everything that acts is a cruelty."[212] To be is to be cruel—there is no way out of cruelty, which, however, must be conceived anew: "Cruelty is not just a matter of either sadism or bloodshed, at least not in any exclusive way… [It] must be taken in a broad sense, and not in the rapacious physical sense that is customarily given to it."[213] Although never as clear as Rosset on what this novel understanding of cruelty may be like, Artaud developed a new set of shock- and scandal-filled stage techniques and communication devices, i.e. his *Theatre of Cruelty*, which was aimed at eliciting higher levels of personal awareness in the audience: "All this culminates in consciousness and torment, and in consciousness *in* torment".[214]

Intrinsically

In the second group are included those thinkers that have argued that cruelty might be intrinsically valuable, maybe even a virtue, which enriches our lives in a unique way and allows for the full realization of our nature. The most 'in-famous' example in this sense is that of the Marquis de Sade, who argues: "Cruelty is imprinted within the animals... that can read the laws of Nature much more energetically than we do; [cruelty] is more strongly enacted by Nature among the savages than it is among civilized men: it would be absurd to establish that it is a kind of depravity".[215] Sade, who approves also of more refined forms of cruelty (i.e. the civilised libertine's), infers from the naturalness and unavoidability of cruelty a reversed Rousseauvianism:

> *Remove your laws, your punishments, your customs, and cruelty will not have dangerous effects any longer... it is inside the civilized domain that it turns into a danger, as those capable of it are almost always absent, either because they lack the force, or because they lack the means to respond to the offences; in the uncivilized domain, instead, if it is imposed over the strong, then he shall be able to react to it, and if it is imposed over the weak, it will not be else than conceding to the strong according to the laws of nature, and this will not be inappropriate at all.*[216]

Equally notorious is the case of Friedrich Nietzsche, whom the reader has already met repeatedly in this book. Idealising and idolising primeval societies, barbaric bravery and warrior mores, Nietzsche wishes to:

> *[E]mpathise with those tremendous eras of "morality of custom" which precede "world history" as the actual and decisive eras of history which determined the character of mankind: the eras in which suffering counted as virtue, cruelty counted as virtue, dissembling counted as virtue,*

revenge counted as virtue, denial of reason counted as virtue, while on the other hand well-being was accounted a danger, desire for knowledge was accounted a danger, peace was accounted a danger, pity was accounted a danger, being pitied was accounted an affront, work was accounted an affront, madness was accounted godliness, and change was accounted immoral and pregnant with disaster![217]

If Sade reverses Rousseau's *bon sauvage* [noble savage (the term was never used by him, but is commonly associated with him)], Nietzsche reverses Seneca's treatment of cruelty as vice. For Nietzsche, cruelty used to be a virtue in prehistoric or barbaric times, it is a fixed element in the human make-up, and it survives in countless rarefied forms today:

Cruelty is what constitutes the painful sensuality of tragedy. And what pleases us in so-called tragic pity as well as in everything sublime, up to the highest and most delicate of metaphysical tremblings, derives its sweetness exclusively from the intervening component of cruelty. Consider the Roman in the arena, Christ in the rapture of the cross, the Spaniard at the sight of the stake or the bullfight, the present-day Japanese flocking to tragedies, the Parisian suburban laborer who is homesick for bloody revolutions, the Wagnerienne who unfastens her will and lets Tristan und Isolde "wash over her" – what they all enjoy and crave with a mysterious thirst to pour down their throats is "cruelty," the spiced drink of the great Circe.[218]

Given all this, as Nietzsche concludes, cruelty should be recovered in an honest and healthy way, for human beings are cruelty-prone animals that live in the mundane world, not the God-like, spiritualised, 'fallen' and heaven-seeking creatures of which religion and philosophy have pointlessly blared about for centuries. Just like all other animals, so do human beings have bodies, selfish selves, and 'knightly' instincts calling for competition, predation and domination. Humans are born to race against one another and the most deserving ones, in the end, ought to survive and lead. Any departure from this natural logic is a concession to degeneration and, essentially, an unhealthily indirect manifestation of repressed cruelty, which cannot but harm our species by letting slaves dominate over masters, priests over knights, and ignorant masses over cultured elites. Instead of understanding and embracing the cruel but actual reality of the world, which is the only place where true existential meaning can be found, the degenerate pursue mystification and escapism. Exemplarily, the loathed magician/pope of Nietzsche's grand and initially ill-received philosophical allegory, i.e. his 1883–91 *Thus Spoke Zarathustra: A Book for All and None*, discovers this hard truth in his delirium, as he realises that his own pantheon of abstract instruments of power (angels, demons, God, etc.) is the utmost and most cruel betrayal of any chance for real fulfilment. Nothing of what he has been preaching during his life, in order to lead his flock, is true and truly valuable: *"In vain! / Pierce further! / Cruellest spike! / No dog – your game just am I, / Cruellest hunter! / .../ Speak finally! / You shrouded in the lightning! Unknown! Speak! /.../ Surrender to me, / Cruellest enemy, / - Yourself!"*[219]

Concluding Remarks

Nietzsche's virtue has hardly anything to do with Seneca's vice. The five conceptions of cruelty presented above differ too much from one another to be able to provide any one clear set of guidelines about the role that cruelty can or should play *vis-à-vis* any desired development of human life. The family resemblances suggested in the third section leave the field open to many diverging paths, which reflect not only the dissimilar interpretations of cruelty, but also the various presuppositions and conceptions that the cited authors have concerning human life as such, the opportunities, and the means of its development, not to mention the uneven ontological, cosmological, theological and ethical commitments that they are willing to promote. Nevertheless, there is value in plurality. Each conception offers a conspicuous amount of food for thought.

If cruelty is a vice, for example, then we can attribute and claim responsibility for it and for the sort of person that we are. If cruelty is sadism, however, its horror may well remind us that the very same responsibility knows of limitations, possibly due to social and pathological factors. And if these factors can be modified, then much could and should be done to prevent and reduce cruelty. Certainly, there may be divergences regarding the fundamental values that ought to guide these modifications, whether at the individual or at the collective level. Besides, we may also come to realise, like Artaud and Hallie did, that cruelty possesses a paradoxical dimension, i.e. that cruelty can only be reduced and not eliminated *in toto*. We might even want to avoid its comprehensive elimination as a desirable goal, for there may be select cruelties capable of enriching life. Moreover, embracing the cruel character of existence might serve itself as a precondition for any meaningful life to be lived. Avoiding the hopelessness, the self-pity and the negative nihilism of, say, Arthur Schopenhauer, who dreamed of utter annihilation (i.e. Buddhist nirvana) as the supreme wisdom, we may want to side at least with Leopardi's pessimism, which found enough value in life by way of the stoical ability to contemplate cruel reality for what it is. Or we may prefer another, less austere option. The extent of the embrace is not easy to measure—perhaps it is impossible to measure; or it varies with each and everyone's 'arm-span'.

Certainly, Sade and Nietzsche went very far. The former's sophisticated hedonistic libertine and the latter's knightly blond beast are *prima facie* unlikely heroes; it is improbable that the readers of this book would truly like to encounter them in their life. More likely, they might enjoy being such characters, as the fascination with murderous villains seems to suggest, whether in the medieval version of the saga-inspiring Egill Skallagrímsson or the contemporary one of the computer-generated criminals of *Grand Theft Auto*. Individual daydreaming is one thing, however, and collective life is another. Which balance is to be found between the two, whilst striving for aesthetic self-realisation on the one hand and for justice on the other, is the dilemma that Richard Rorty refused to solve for us. Each one of us, he believed, must find the solution by and for herself.

Chapter 5: The Politics of Cruelty: On Sade and Nietzsche

The present chapter offers a succinct comparative study of the philosophical considerations on the nature and function of cruelty given by the Marquis de Sade and Friedrich Nietzsche. As such, this chapter is meant to serve three main purposes: (1) it provides a more detailed account of the understanding of cruelty in the philosophies of these two thinkers, thus highlighting, albeit not probing further, a major axiological dimension involved in the moral assessment of cruelty; (2) it adds to the rather thin body of studies in philosophy and in the history of ideas dealing specifically with cruelty; and (3) it develops a comparison between their two philosophies, thus deepening the understanding of a striking case of intellectual affinity, which has been recognised by many but studied by few.[220]

Cruelty in Sade's Philosophy

The starting point of Sade's reflections is the understanding of cruelty as the most ordinary given of human life in the state of nature and, precisely because of this natural ordinariness, as the most valuable. We read in the previous chapter how Sade argues, in his *Philosophy in the Bedroom*, that:

Cruelty is imprinted within the animals... that can read the laws of nature much more energetically than we do; it is more strongly enacted by nature among the savages than it is among civilized men: it would be absurd to establish that it is a kind of depravity... Cruelty is nothing but the human energy that civilization has not yet corrupted: it is therefore a virtue and not a vice... Cruelty, far from being a vice, is the first sentiment that Nature has imprinted within ourselves. The child breaks his toy, bites his nurse's nipple, strangles his bird, long before he has reached the age of reason.

Cruelty is, for Sade, a fundamental form of energy—however vaguely defined this concept is in his philosophy—that initiates and informs human agency in its most basic manifestations. The same passages also indicate how Sade takes for self-evident that reason ought not to interfere with this "first sentiment", for he claims that tampering with such a powerful natural endowment of ours is tantamount to its corruption. Animals and savages, who are closer to this primeval source of self-expression, are taken to be exemplars of what consistent and uncorrupted children of nature are like. In Sade's universe, Rousseau's noble savage turns into a cruel savage.

Sade's appreciation for the primeval conditions of life displayed by animals and savages does not imply that no trace of the instinct of cruelty is left in the civilised world. On the contrary, such a world would not even exist, were it not for the ongoing exchange of mutual cruelties between the mighty and the weak, "usurpation" being for Sade the regulative principle of human coexistence in all societies. As we read in *Juliette*:

> *When going back to the origin of the right to property, one reaches necessarily usurpation. In this case theft is not punished as it establishes the right to property; but the right itself is originally nothing but a theft itself: as a consequence the law punishes the theft of that which is itself a theft, the weak who tries to regain his due, and the mighty who wants to found or increase his own, taking advantage of that which he has received from nature.*[221]

Nature has created human beings unequal, and, for Sade, it is the most obvious consequence that the more gifted—the "mighty" individual—takes advantage of this situation of disparity in skill and in capacity for self-affirmation. Still, as Sade admits, it follows from the same principle of "usurpation" that "the weak" should try to regain the possessions lost to "the mighty". Equalising counter-theft by "the weak" is the natural response to the initial act of theft by "the mighty", and the struggle between the two alternately usurping parties is what keeps the social balance going throughout human history:

> *[T]he mighty has taken possession of everything, hence the defect in nature's balance; the weak defends himself and robs the mighty: here are the crimes that establish the necessary equilibrium of nature... If the mighty seems to be causing disorder by stealing to the one who is beneath him, the weak re-establishes it by stealing to his superiors, and both serve nature.*[222]

In the third chapter of the present book we saw how Cesare Beccaria, another son of the celebrated century of the Enlightenment, had already acknowledged the "cruel and perhaps unnecessary right to property" and its perplexing connection with the crime of theft, from which ensue "atrocious" penal cruelties. Sade too seems to be fully aware of this critical insight, although he gives a very peculiar twist to it. Beccaria was always troubled by this notion on moral and social grounds, and proposed detailed programmes for institutional and legal reform aimed at reducing the likelihood of the most dramatic outcomes related to property and theft, i.e. crime and punishment.

Unlike Beccaria, Sade was ready to accept wholeheartedly this cruel system of "usurpation" in its blunt mercilessness, as it does nothing else but mirror most candidly the inner logic of nature itself. For Sade, rather, the problem is that civilisation can be hypocritical about this regulating principle of "usurpation", insofar as the civilised person denies that cruelty sits at the core of social coexistence and, whilst employing it, prevents its unrestrained expression. Sade abhors the fact that the civilised person creates intellectual and institutional façades hiding the sorry truth and distorting its flow. By doing so, the civilised person favours theft and hampers counter-theft: because of this mechanism of deception and self-deception, the logic of "usurpation" is prevented from unfolding along the path intended by nature.

In Sade's understanding, the act of denial, the prevention of counter-theft, and the consequent corruption of nature's cruel *logos* [inherent logic] are caused typically by three fictional structures of deception and self-deception that characterise of human civilisation: morals, laws, and religion. Instead of accepting openly the struggle of "usurpation", the civilised person uses them *qua* instituted cunning and inculcated falsity to seemingly escape from it gaining, in the process, an unfair, unnatural advantage. As Sade quips: "I like listening to these wealthy people, titled people, these magistrates, these priests... I like seeing them preach us virtue. It is very difficult to protect oneself from theft, when one has three times more than it is needed to live!"[223]

Acting in this manner, not only does the civilised person negate hypocritically the reality of things, i.e. that cruelty is still at work within her allegedly reformed and humane institutions, but also does "the mighty" turn into "the weak", for she becomes afraid of being tested, i.e. she does not face bravely the reaction of "the weak" to her initial action of "usurpation", since this action is not recognised for what it is any longer. Relentlessly, weakness creeps inside the universe of "the mighty" herself, hence endangering her natural disposition toward cruelty: "You tell us about a chimerical impulse of this nature, which orders us not to do to other what we would not want to be done to us; but this absurd suggestion has come only from men – and weak men. The powerful man shall never try to speak such a language."[224] For Sade, as we read in the previous chapter, the remedy to this situation is straightforward: abate all laws, all punishments, all emasculating mores, and let out in the open all hypocritically hidden cruelty, so that the natural order may be re-established. Sade advocates a profoundly selfish naturalist axiological dogma, which anticipates much social Darwinism and Objectivism of the following centuries, and claims: "the mighty can exploit the weak as much as she wishes", for such is "the order of nature" or "general law" that humans must not "destroy".[225] Nature ought to be left free to run along its course, in order to avoid the impoverishment of human character and the worsening of our species' skills and capabilities: "Cruelty is in nature; we are all born

81

with a dose of cruelty that is up to education to modify; but education is not in nature, and it is as damaging to the sacred effects of nature as cultivation is to trees… the tree abandoned to the whims of nature is more beautiful and produces better fruits."[226] Cruelty is, for Sade, much more than just the rather vaguely defined fundamental energy of our species: it is the energy fostering life itself in its productive manifestations, which Sade characterises both aesthetically (wild "trees" being "more beautiful") and biologically (wild "trees" producing "better fruits", whether botanically correct or not).

In order to provide a model for the re-naturalised human being to come, Sade populates his pornographic novels with peculiar heroes and heroines. Propensity to crime, blasphemy, 'unnatural' sexual acts (i.e. expressions of natural desires that are hypocritically condemned by society, tribunals and priests) and *immoralia* [immoral acts] of all sorts are the main features of these ideal types. Such scandalous libertines exemplify the radical reaction against the three pillars of civilised cruelty deplored by Sade, i.e. morals, laws and religion. Consistently, trying to popularise his philosophical views, Sade chose the most violent pornography *qua* literary vehicle. The potent activation of our felt being by means of artistic representations that are *horribile visu* [horrible to see] is, in fact, the first step toward the recovery of our original energy:

> *We want to be entertained, it is the goal of all men who free themselves to voluptuousness, and we want to be entertained in the most active ways… It does not matter to know whether our means will be pleasant or unpleasant to the object that we use, that which matters is to activate the complex of our nerves via the most violent shock possible.*[227]

Sade's message could not be any clearer: give us horror, give us blood, give us sex, and, in a *crescendo* [lit. growing, increasing; in music, getting gradually louder and louder] of sensorial stimulation, do not worry if somebody gets hurt. Indeed, to those who still wonder "whether it is charitable to hurt another to enjoy oneself",

Sade replies by stressing the individualistic character of human existence which, by embracing sadism, abides by nature's own command:

What do to us the pains produced onto our neighbour? Do we feel them? No, on the contrary... their production crystallizes into a delightful sensation for us. Why should we spare an individual that does not have any connection with us? For which reason should we spare him a pain that is never going to cause us any harm, when it is certain that we are going to derive great pleasure from it? Have we ever felt a single natural impulse suggesting us that we should prefer somebody else to ourselves, and is not each of us alone in the world?[228]

Sade wants the human being to be in harmony with nature's cruel yet sacred *logos*:

Nature, our common mother, does never talk to us of anything else but ourselves; nothing is so selfish as her voice and we recognize therein the most candid... and saint counsel that we should enjoy ourselves, no matter whom is going to pay for it. But the others, you may say, could seek revenge... At the end of the day, the mightiest alone will be right.[229]

Sade follows the standard Enlightenment's relinquishment of traditional religion and mores, as well as the scientific naturalistic reduction of humankind to the level of animals; but he also brings them to a paradoxical conclusion, for Sade discovers the heart of darkness throbbing within our breast that the old religion and mores, and the belief in the higher status of humankind *vis-à-vis* other animal species, had been trying to 'civilise'. Praising instead all that is 'uncivil', from wild trees to primitive societies, Sade claims this terrible *logos* to be inscribed within our own bodies and in our deepest instincts, which must be given free rein for the sake of a healthy natural development:

83

Our constitution, our organs, the flows of the humours, the
energy of the animal spirits, here are the physical causes that
make us be... Titus or Nero, Messalina or Chantal; one
should not be proud for his virtue and contrite for his vice,
nor should one accuse nature for having us been born good
or evil; she has acted according to her views, her plans and
needs: let us surrender to her.[230]

Cruelty in Nietzsche's Philosophy

In the previous chapters, we surveyed significant passages from
Nietzsche's *Ecce Homo, Genealogy of Morals, Daybreak* and
Beyond Good and Evil, all of which point towards the notion that
cruelty persists in diverse and elaborate forms in civilised life.
Parallel to Sade's upside-down Rousseauvianism stands Nietzsche's
recognition of the fact that civilisation has been tampering with this
instinct, hence corrupting human nature, despite its being fuelled by
cruelty at a most fundamental level.

A first way in which this corruption has occurred is the
hypocritical denial of the actual presence of cruelty within the
civilised *polis* [the ancient Greek urban polity]. Like Sade, also
Nietzsche accuses morals, laws, and religion of being paramount
exemplars of collective and individual self-deception, which twist
the perception of brute force into that of commendable behaviour:

In conditions obtaining before the existence of the state the
individual can act harshly and cruelly for the purpose of
frightening other creatures: to secure his existence through
such fear-inspiring tests of his power. Thus does the man of
violence, of power, the original founder of states, act when he
subjugates the weaker... Morality is preceded by compulsion,
indeed it is for a time itself still compulsion, to which one
accommodates oneself for the avoidance of what one regards
as unpleasurable. Later it becomes custom, later still
voluntary obedience, finally almost instinct: then, like all that

has for a long time been habitual and natural, it is associated
with pleasure - and is now called virtue.[231]

Moralists, legislators and priests, according to Nietzsche's reconstruction of human history, employ regularly a fraudulent lexicon that was not in use in the warrior past of our race. Originally, the Tables of the Law were written directly on the flesh of the human being. Today, instead, allegedly 'high' and abstract justifications make cruelty's face disappear under the categories of ethical imperatives, constitutions and legal requirements, though at a deeper level of scrutiny, each person's

> *right to [be cruel] is the same as the state now relegates to itself; or rather, there exists no right that can prevent this from happening. The ground for any kind of morality can then be prepared only when a greater individual or a collective individuality, for example society, the state, subjugates all other individuals, that is to say draws them out of their isolation and orders them within a collective.*[232]

Cruelty lingers on at the very core of the institutionalised morality called "The Law": it may be negated *de iure* [in theory], but it is *de facto* [in practice] employed, *in iure* [in the law] itself.

The theoretical split envisaged by Nietzsche between appearance (i.e. "virtue") and reality (i.e. "compulsion") reflects the psychological split lurking behind the hypocritical convictions of the modern human being, who believes that she has freed herself from the ancient burden of cruelty, whilst she is in fact an active carrier of it. Thus, "political sectarians are treated harshly and cruelly, but because one has learned to believe in the necessity of the state one is not as sensible of the cruelty as one is in the former case, where we repudiate the ideas behind it."[233] For Nietzsche, a false consciousness resides at the core of the moral lexicon of the civilised world, and a kind of schizophrenia characterises the civilised human being, who enacts all sorts of cruelties whilst denying her own responsibility in and for them, blaming them instead on the complex hierarchies within and through which she lives and operates: "Much that is horrific and inhuman in history in which one can hardly bear to believe is... [such] that he who ordered it and he who carried it out are different people: the former does not see it and his imagination therefore receives no strong impression of it, the latter obeys one set above him and does not feel responsible."[234]

Christianity is, in Sade's view, a most significant example of the hypocritical corruption of our primeval animal instincts, and one that developed over few centuries of recorded world history upon the older basis of Jewish monotheistic beliefs, i.e. the priestly and self-soothing religion of a marginal Middle-Eastern nation, who experienced defeat and servitude on many occasions. According to Nietzsche's understanding of the Christian faith, it is within this peculiar religious context that the figure of the priestly person comes to contradict and defy the figure of the knightly person, i.e. the primitive warrior, the Babylonian conqueror or the Homeric hero. *Ressentiment* [envious and enervating resentment (Nietzsche uses intentionally the semantically richer French term)] prospers in the priestly person's heart, for not only does she dislike that which was formerly considered virtuous and noble, but also because she wants to transform the entire universe, to 'pacify' it by making it her own, in an attempt to 'rescue' it from its cruel nature—as though such a transformation were possible. The priestly person cannot confront openly "the sorry scheme of things" in which she dwells, as Nietzsche characterises it in *The Greek State*; this scheme being regulated by an inherent and inescapable *logos* of cruel destruction and regeneration that the priestly person cannot master. Instead, the priestly person follows the road of deception and self-deception.

New, hidden, unnatural and unhealthily perverted cruelty is bound to emerge in the fanciful and allegedly cruelty-free context that the priestly person so creates:

[I]t is imagined that the gods too are refreshed and in festive mood when they are offered the spectacle of cruelty – and thus there creeps into the world the idea that voluntary suffering, self-chosen torture, is meaningful and valuable...

86

All those spiritual leaders of the peoples who were able to stir something into motion within the inert but fertile mud of their customs have, in addition to madness, also had need of voluntary torture if they were to inspire belief – and first and foremost, as always, their own belief in themselves! The more their spirit ventured on to new paths and was as a consequence tormented by pangs of conscience and spasms of anxiety, the more cruelly did they rage against their own flesh, their own appetites and their own health – as though to offer the divinity a substitute pleasure in case he might perhaps be provoked by this neglect of and opposition to established usages and by the new goals these paths led to.[235]

Rather than aspiring to the natural richness of knightly values, the priestly person sets a new, perverted path to follow, which is disconnected from nature, from mundane reality, from the many more centuries of unrecorded prehistorical evolution of our species and from the true necessities of life—and which is "deep down... Emptiness."[236] The priestly person, for Nietzsche, explores "the ways of self-narcotisation", such as "intoxication as cruelty in the tragic enjoyment of the destruction of the noblest... resignation to generalizing about oneself, a pathos; mysticism, the voluptuous enjoyment of eternal emptiness."[237] The priestly person is incapable of looking at "the cruel and desolate face of nature", which constitutes, *au contraire* [on the contrary], the knightly person's supreme awareness.[238] In effect, the priestly person takes revenge on this awareness. She creates phantoms like the Heavens and the Real World past the earthly one, both of which are tragic parodies of what she would have liked to enjoy in the only world that is given, had she not been so weak as not to be able to attain it: "The sick and perishing—it was they who despised the body and the earth, and invented the heavenly world, and the redeeming blood-drops; but even those sweet and sad poisons they borrowed from the body and the earth!".[239]

Consequent to this failure is the fact that a deeply rooted frustration, more than any other emotion, drives the actions of the priestly person, including the outer projections of her inner dissatisfaction, under the guise of an unattainable ideal of other-worldly perfection that mocks the perfection of this world. Thus, the priestly person sacrifices the one and only real world to her discontent-inspired fictions, and generates the conditions for the utmost corruption of human nature.[39] 'Modern' and secular versions of this priestly self-denial lead this attitude to their most extreme consequences, such as 19th-century positivists, who sacrifice all meaning to the idols of "rocks, stupidity, gravity, fate, or nothingness out of sheer cruelty to themselves"; their unaware internalisation of centuries of "religious cruelty" making them believe that their "worship" of scientifically described dust, devoid of any genuine existential significance, is the highest point of civilisation and a sign of intellectual superiority, while it is in fact to "sacrifice God for nothingness".[240]

Nietzsche rejects this ill, self-deluding human type, and exalts the fierce, knightly human being of the ancient times, when hypocrisy had not yet flourished, and the instinct of cruelty had not yet been perverted. Such an ilk of persons could really stare life in the eye, accept it in its terrifying beauty, and fight on. Nothing is more enchanting, in Nietzsche's accounts of human vicissitudes, than

> the magnificent blond beast avidly prowling round for spoil and victory... Roman, Arabian, Germanic, Japanese nobility, Homeric heroes, Scandinavian Vikings... their unconcern and scorn for safety, body, life, comfort, their shocking cheerfulness and depth of delight in all destruction, in all the debauches of victory and cruelty... [and] the magnificent but at the same time so shockingly violent world of Homer.[241]

Like Sade did before him, so does Nietzsche derive from such a dramatic view of the cosmos the imperative according to which all instincts, however bestial they may look, ought to be endorsed and allowed to produce their natural effects: "Do I counsel you to slay your instincts? I counsel you the innocence in your instincts."[242] To resist the instincts implanted by nature within ourselves is to take the road to malaise. Cruelty, when it is not heroically lived *in foro externo* [in the public sphere], becomes a devious tyrant *in foro interno* [within oneself]. The realisation of the intrinsic bestiality of the human being should discourage the priestly type's futile and sickening pursuit, for it is only by resuscitating our fullness of being that life becomes healthy, meaningful, and beautiful: "Not when the truth is filthy, but when it is shallow, doth the discerning one go unwillingly into its waters."[243] Under this respect, plain and clear selfishness, to the point of sadism, pervades Nietzsche's own admiration of the knightly figure, as he argues that nature itself has designed our bodies to be self-centredly cruel: "As far as our nervous system extends we guard ourselves against pain: if it extended further, namely into our fellow men, we would never do harm to another (except in such cases as when we do it to ourselves, that is to say when we cut ourselves for the purpose of a cure, exert and weary ourselves for the sake of our health)."[244] Yet, as we all know, we are more than capable of doing harm to others, whose exact "*degree* of pain" suffered "is in any event unknown to us."[245]

Critical Remarks on Sade

Sade's characterisation of cruelty possesses so much rhetorical force as it lacks careful critical analysis. This is not uncommon in the philosophical literature about cruelty at large, which regularly relies upon the commonsensical understanding of the term and presupposes its obvious badness. This very same badness is that which Sade and Nietzsche are actually glad to exploit to their benefit, i.e. in order to shock their bourgeois readership by sounding radical in their assertion of amorality—beyond good and evil. This common vagueness notwithstanding, further contradictions mine Sade's treatment of the concept of cruelty, which I consider most revealing of the fundamental axiological dimension lurking behind his philosophical considerations.

First of all, the distinction between 'bad' and 'good' cruelty does not appear solely with respect to Sade's rejection of corrupting civilisation for the sake of nature's better order. Perplexingly, in Sade's *Philosophy in the Bedroom*, we read:

> *We distinguish two types of cruelty... [the former] originates from stupidity and, involving no reason or analysis, makes the individual that was born like this similar to a wild beast... [This type of cruelty] does not provide any pleasure, for the one who is prone to it does not search for any refinement... [The latter type of cruelty] is the result of the sensitivity of the organs, it is known only to extremely delicate beings, and the excesses it generates are nothing else than refinements of their delicateness; it is this delicateness that employs all the resources of cruelty to alert itself, as it vanishes too easily because of its fineness.* [246]

This statement is at odds with the understanding of cruelty given throughout the rest of the novel—and of his writings in general. Predominantly, Sade argues in favour of the renunciation of all forms of cultivation of the spirit and *pro* [in favour of] the full-fledged return to nature's prime and primeval law of "usurpation". In this passage, instead, Sade seems to be suggesting that the cruelty to be praised more is the one involving calculated sophistication, rather than natural, animal spontaneity. Indeed, in Sade's *Philosophy in the Bedroom*, we also find a scene where the innocent Eugénie is being taught by an exquisitely refined libertine about how to be "careful about your reputation and, without letting anybody be suspicious... [acquire] the art of doing that pleases you most."[247]

Perhaps, Sade's inverted Rousseauvianism cannot exclude completely some other forms of satisfactory adherence to the principle of "usurpation". Furthermore, Sade appears to be taking nature at face value, thus never reconsidering his characterisation of it, which speaks only of brutish violence and of selfish interest, and leaves no room for tranquillity and altruism. *Contra* Sade, it could be argued that such benign determinations are also present within nature's scope. Rousseau's luminous understanding of nature may not be completely right, but it cannot be denied either that it appears to contain some elements of truth, which Sade blocks out *a priori* [prior to direct experience or empirical scrutiny].

The chief problem is that Sade looks at the universe from the perspective of cruelty alone, and cannot see anything that is not untainted by it. Yet, in his more personal writings, a different picture of the world can be excavated. In his prison letters, for example, we find Sade lamenting about the inhumane cruelty suffered by himself and by his fellow inmates: "Here is nothing in the universe that concerns me or interests me like my release from this abominable place where men are treated like wild beasts and, which is worse, by their fellow men."[248] Why should the advocate of "usurpation" complain about such a treatment? Consistently with his views on artificial cruelty, penal institutions should not exist; but why is Sade complaining about the guards' callousness to the prisoners? Aren't they just serving nature by taking advantage of their position of superiority and by showing no mercy to the inmates? Unless we take the long philosophical monologues of his numerous remorseless libertines as sheer novelistic fiction, then Sade should here invoke revolt, adhering to the cruel principles of nature's order. Following nature, "the weak" ought to strike back against "the mighty"—a response which, to be honest, Sade did pursue in first person and, to some extent, achieved, by having scandalous plays of his staged by fellow inmates, by publishing his pornographic-philosophical novels despite official prohibitions and court injunctions, and by joining the ranks of the most radical French revolutionaries to bring forth political equality.

An analogous contradiction appears in Sade's political writings, in which he dreams of the city Paris becoming "the bane of despots, the temple of the arts, the motherland of all free men."[249] Sade, despite his aristocratic lineage, joined wholeheartedly the forces of the Revolution against the privileges of the nobility and, even more ardently, against those of the clergy. This move would have been consistent with his views on cruelty if he had condemned the *ancien régime* [old regime, i.e. before the French Revolution] for preventing cruelty from flowing freely according to the laws of nature. However, that was not the reason that he gave, at least publicly. On the contrary, Sade condemned "religion" for its "cruelty", and for being "an inexhaustible source of murders and crimes… invented by men's infamy, which has no other goal but to deceive them or to arm them against each other."[250] In their place, Sade spoke in favour of "filial piety, greatness of soul, courage, equality, good faith, love of the fatherland", i.e. in favour of all "the virtues… to become the only objects of our veneration."[251]

In conclusion, there exists a fracture separating Sade the novelist and philosopher of libertinage from Sade the man and enthusiastic *citoyen* [citizen] of the first French Republic. This fracture makes Sade appear like an upside-down Schopenhauer: whereas Schopenhauer preached compassion in the face of nature's inherent cruelty and behaved selfishly, Sade preached selfishness in the name of the same nature and, yet, behaved compassionately.

Critical Remarks on Nietzsche

Nietzsche's treatment of cruelty is not less richly rhetorical and poorly analytical than Sade's. Nor does it display fewer internal tensions, which, as it was already the case with Sade, I believe capable of disclosing interesting information about the ultimate ground of value lurking behind their reflections concerning cruelty.

To begin, Nietzsche's admiration for the barbaric societies of the ancient times is the most evident sign of his exclusivist attitude in social matters, especially when it is formulated as the appreciation of the hierarchical organisation of society: "We must accept this cruel sounding truth, that slavery is of the essence of Culture… This truth is the vulture, that gnaws at the liver of the Promethean promoter of Culture…[62] The misery of toiling men must still increase in order to make the production of the world of art possible to a small number of Olympian men."[252] For Nietzsche, if we want beauty to have any chance to blossom within the *polis*, then hierarchical domination and outright exploitation must be carried forth without restriction and without remorse. The elected few can enjoy a life full of frenzy and of intensity of experience, if and only if the many are enslaved to labour for their sake. Aesthetic perfection presupposes political cruelty. This is why Nietzsche fears "the secret wrath nourished by Communists and Socialists of all times, and also by their feebler descendants, the white race of the 'Liberals,' not only against the arts, but also against classical antiquity".[253] Nietzsche is adamantly sceptical of the many self-appointed 'modernisers' who, if his psychological analyses are correct, are motivated, perhaps subconsciously, by envious and enervating resentment to all and every vestige of aristocratic superiority, and therefore promote 'priestly' political programmes of alleged 'liberation' of the masses, teaching 'useful' subjects with 'practical' applications in mind, and fostering a universal levelling that "would be the cry of compassion tearing down the walls of Culture".[254]

Nietzsche's uncompromising stance for the aristocracy of the spirit sounds definitely unilateral, and it could not sound differently, for it is based upon an equally unilateral and aristocratic interpretation of nature. Under this respect, Nietzsche's worldview is strikingly analogous to Sade's, insofar as both of them depict nature along socio-Darwinist lines (truly *ante litteram*, in Sade's case). For them both, nature is a vicious battleground where the naturally gifted superior few must clash with the naturally resentful inferior many, as it was essentially still argued by Herbert Spencer (1820–1903), who coined the expression "survival of the fittest",[255] Adolf Hitler (1889–1945), *per* his notorious but rarely studied book *Mein Kampf*,[256] and Ayn Rand (1902–1982), who is today one of the most influential philosophers among US conservatives.[257] Perhaps, such a view is correct in many a respect, but it seems to ignore blatantly the common traits that the few share with the many, not to mention the plausible Rousseauvian, benign and cooperative colours that nature may also possess. This issue becomes particularly controversial if we consider that Nietzsche does not reject *in toto* the possibility that human instincts can be moulded and mis-moulded. Conditioning, however unhealthy it may be, can be a powerful tool by which to shape and re-shape both individual souls and collective cultures. This does not mean solely that cruelty cannot be eradicated. More dramatically, it also means that cruelty can be instilled within otherwise merciful souls, as Nietzsche himself suggests in a rare passage from *Human, All Too Human*:

> *Whether or not our passions glow red hot and direct the whole course of our life depends on whether or not we have had certain painfully affecting sights and impressions – a father unjustly condemned, killed or tortured, for example, an unfaithful wife, a cruel attack by an enemy. No one knows whither circumstances, pity, indignation may drive him, no one knows the degree of his inflammability. Paltry little circumstances make one paltry oneself; it is usually not the quality of his experiences but their quantity that distinguishes the lower from the higher man, in both good and evil.*[258]

To this, Nietzsche adds:

> *Indeed, no cruel man is so cruel as he whom he has misused believes; the idea of pain is not the same thing as the suffering of it. The same applies to the unjust judge, to the journalist who misleads public opinion with petty untruths. Cause and effect are in all these cases surrounded by quite different groups of thoughts and sensations; while one involuntarily presupposes that doer and sufferer think and feel the same and, in accordance with this presupposition, assesses the guilt of the one by the pain of the other.*[259]

These remarks carry with themselves an unseen challenge to Nietzsche's admiration for the mores of the ancient hero, insofar as the hero would appear unable to perceive the pain and/or shock that his ruthless actions cause the victim to experience. To be cruel, then, would not be a sign of particular strength, but of empathic inability, as commonly recorded among pathological bullies and sociopaths. In reality, then, the intensity of experience pertaining to being cruel would not be so high as it was being suggested by Nietzsche in his other cited passages, for the hero's *telos* [defining goal] of domination turns out to be a trivial task that can be easily complied

94

with. No particularly exciting challenge is left in Nietzsche's version of Sade's "usurpation", if we follow the logic implied by these generally neglected remarks of the former, for the undertaking at issue requires simply that the stronger, naturally rapacious, lupine, knightly person, must prey upon the weaker, perceptually removed, ovine, priestly person. In truth, as Nietzsche himself writes, the pain of the latter is so separated from the perception of the former, that "the individual [can be] disposed like an annoying insect", i.e. something that even a child could do, and, most probably, without much thrill.[260]

Concluding Remarks

The main line of argument about cruelty of both Sade and Nietzsche can be synthesised as follows: [a] cruelty is a natural *datum* [given] and, nature being intrinsically good, it is henceforth a good one; [b] it is a powerful natural *datum*, which cannot but be there, for it operates behind all animal activities, including the human ones, hence it is bound to burst through any alleged 'civilised' boundary or supposed 'overcoming' of it; [c] its operations can unravel either openly or secretly and, correspondingly, either healthily or unhealthily; [d] the mightiest examples of healthy expression of this *datum* in the context of human interactions are those of iron-fisted self-affirmation, candid immorality, brave criminality, and similar (puzzling) expressions of utmost individual vitality.

It must be highlighted that neither Sade nor Nietzsche provides any precise definition of cruelty. Mostly, they outline general traits revealing the presence of a form of fundamental energy rooted within the most basic natural drives. Without it, no self-affirmation would be possible, whether on an individual scale or on a collective scale. Cruelty appears to be part of, if not even the whole of, a cosmic *logos* of generation, destruction and regeneration, e.g. Sade's logic of "usurpation" and Nietzsche's natural *Werden* [becoming, being-in-motion] of "begetting, living, and murdering" that he inherits from Schopenhauer. As such, cruelty can be either good or bad. It is good insofar as it follows its natural path, i.e. as it brings forth new life, though sacrificing some of the old. It is bad insofar as it follows an artificial path, which prevents new life from emerging, and which allows old life to persist in a more and more corrupt state. This persistence interferes with the cosmic *logos*, hence reducing future chances of positive generation and regeneration, e.g. Nietzsche's horror for priestly "self-narcotisation" and metaphysical "emptiness" and Sade's condemnation of human tampering with the freely growing wild "trees".

Life itself, which Sade and Nietzsche connote as intensity of experience (e.g. the libertine's shock of the senses and the warrior's destructive frenzy) and as unrestrained self-affirmation (e.g. Sade's Nero and Nietzsche's conquerors), seems to be the axiological basis upon which their considerations about cruelty rely. Even the puzzlement that the reader may experience whenever she is presented with Sade's and Nietzsche's positive assessment of the most heinous crimes, seems to rely upon the very same axiological basis. It is the destructive side of the cruel *logos* embodied by their heroes that appears to be afflicting us. Something terrible is displayed thereby, i.e. the ruthless elimination of life, even though in the name of further life. The sacrifice of virgins, infants, priestly persons and of "the weak" in general, is that which horrifies so much —the sacrifice of life, no matter how 'inferior' and 'worthless' it may be. In brief,. life would appear to be the ground of value upon which dwells the positive and/or negative assessment of cruelty.

Besides, the experience of sheer horror itself, which the reader may have when entertaining the terrible scenes of depravity depicted by Sade and Nietzsche, can teach us that the cruel frenzy of life, which so important a role plays in both Sade's and Nietzsche's philosophies, may not be the only way in which life is to be understood. Lower degrees of intensity may be preferred to higher ones, in order to enjoy more of them and more often. In other terms, their conception of life is merely *vertical*, insofar as both Sade and Nietzsche are concerned with reaching the most voluptuous heights of aesthetic frenzy and utmost vitality. Still, there is a *horizontal* element to be considered as well, at which they seem to hint with their contradictions, and which they sacrifice blindly to the vertical element, thus causing perplexity and moral disapproval to emerge in their readers (or, at least, in me). The dialectical interplay between the vertical and horizontal dimensions of life is not totally absent from their works. Nonetheless, the dominant line of argument that they follow seems oblivious to it. It is only marginal to their main philosophical considerations, however, that Sade and Nietzsche present us with a notion that life 'horizontally' intended. This one, in which we all share for our own meaningful existence, may require preservation by avoiding just the dangerous disruption involved in living 'vertically' to the point of libertine vice, primeval sadism, or knightly super-humanity. Sade's compassion toward his fellow inmates and his adamant political stance in favour of the Revolution are particularly suggestive in this sense.

Equally significant are Nietzsche's remarks from *Human, All Too Human*, from *The Greek State*, and from the third *Untimely Meditation* about the "cruel and desolate face of nature", i.e. the reality at which the priestly person cannot stare, that "face" being the epiphany of a ruthless "sorry scheme of things" that we cannot change. Nietzsche's choice of adjectives may be episodic and rhetorical, yet it involves nonetheless the recognition of the tragic element of life-destruction entailed by the merciless universe that he portrays in his works. There, Nietzsche seems to recognise that there is a despicable loss of some kind that makes this "scheme of things" a "sorry" one. Of course, Nietzsche is known to have recommended a full acceptance of this 'sorry-ness', by embracing it in a narcissistic act of fusion between the universe and the superior will of the *Übermensch* [super- or beyond-man] that may evolve in the future, after abandoning all old beliefs in any religious or philosophical afterlife or in a better world beyond the present one (e.g. Nietzsche's own fictional Zarathustra). The horizontal factor of life-determination is, in Nietzsche's philosophy, immolated upon the altar of vertical vitality. Whether we may want to follow him along this path, it is open to debate.

As we have seen, not even the infamous "divine Marquis" was really capable of doing it in real life. In conclusion, we are free to appreciate or not the unique exemplars of cruelty populating the writings of Sade and Nietzsche. In either case, their reflections about cruelty are greatly helpful in the individuation of a deep-seated axiological assumption, which operates tacitly beneath their moral and political hermeneutics and, most likely, beneath the reader's as well: the fundamental value of life, the horizontal and vertical components of which are also revealed. For all those who are engaged in the field of value theory, I believe this to be an important result.

Chapter 6: Ordinary Hell. Reflections on Penal Justice between Dante and Nils Christie

Io sono al terzo cerchio, della piova
        etterna maledetta, fredda e greve;
        regola e qualità non l'è nova...
Cerbero, fiera crudele e diversa,
        con tre gole caninamente latra
        sopra la gente che quivi è sommersa.
Li occhi ha vermigli, la barba unta e atra,
        e 'l ventre largo, e unghiate le mani;
        graffia li spirti, scuoia e disquatra.[261]

In the verses above we encounter one of the many gruesome scenes that Dante Alighieri (1265–1321) depicts in his *Comedy*, which Boccaccio (1313–1375) later dubbed "divine"—a predicate that decidedly stuck—or, if we like, we read a report from Dante's nearly unique descent into Hell.[262] As astonishingly crude as it may read, the condition thereby portrayed is nevertheless 'mild', insofar as it describes the eternal punishment inflicted upon the gluttons, namely sinners of the minor type, i.e. those guilty of wanting self-restraint or incontinence. Far more carnage, devastating plagues and torturing devices are at work in the rest of Dante's *Inferno*, where worse types of trespassers are being chastised.[263] Further down, deeper in the profundity of Earth,[264] Virgil shows Dante hordes of desperate souls turned into blood-shedding trees, savagely roasted inside inexhaustible fires, imprisoned in the frozen waters of the *Cocito*, not to mention three souls being chewed mercilessly by Satan.[265] Moreover, since in the *post-mortem* condition everything is more perfect, given the purely spiritual nature of the afterlife, the pain experienced by the damned in their body-like souls is far more intense than anything ever experienced by their ensouled bodies *ante mortem* [before death].[266]

It is important to notice that such a display of *horribilia* [horrible things] is not only the visionary creation of the greatest literary genius of Europe's Middle Ages, but it is also the poetic expression of a commonly accepted belief, namely that a world beyond the present one awaits human souls, either to grant them eternal contentment or to ensure that they are properly castigated. Punishment, however degrading or excruciating it may be, is steadily present along the horizon of the medieval Christian universe as one of the major instruments of divine justice. Indeed, it is still there today for many a Christian, who believe that "the chaff He [God] will burn in a fire that will never go out."[267] To my knowledge, it is not until the 18th Century that this kind of *Weltanschauung* [worldview] started changing significantly, at least beyond small circles of classically educated minds. Only with the dawn of the Enlightenment and the birth of a literate public opinion did this model of human existence start being challenged extensively. Sometimes, this modification meant the abandonment of medieval Christianity *tout-court* [outright]. In other instances, it took the form of an alleged 'rationalisation' or 'modernisation' of the doctrine, both in Catholic and Reformed contexts.[268]

Mainstream Penal Justice

Yet, neither the notion nor the practice of chastisement has subsided with the eclipse of religious belief in the West, nor has the associated characterisation of chastisements, including lawfully justified ones, as inherently painful and plausibly evil. Apart from the verily transparent etymology of "penal", i.e. the Latin word for pain [*poena*], Thomas Hobbes, who was an early-modern materialist, monist, and a possible atheist known to all contemporary scholars in jurisprudence, defined punishment in his *Leviathan* as follows: "A Punishment is an *Evil* inflicted by publique Authority, on him that hath done, or omitted that which is Judged by the same Authority to be a Transgression of the Law."[269] Two centuries later, Jeremy Bentham (1748–1832) was himself to state: "a lot of punishment is a lot of pain... all punishment is mischief: all punishment in itself is *bad*."[270] According to him, the one and only way to make this "evil" acceptable was, perhaps unsurprisingly for the man who coined in the 1780s the term "utilitarianism" itself, that: "On the principle of utility it ought to be allowed only insofar as it promises to exclude some greater evil."[271]

This point by Bentham, by far the influential British champion of utilitarianism, may seem obvious, at least *prima facie*. However, as we saw in the fourth chapter, the moral philosopher Philip P. Hallie would later denounce that the avoidance of a worse evil is the standard justification lurking behind the most atrocious cruelties in human history; as the time-tested adagio recites: "the road to hell is paved with good intentions". On this point, John Kekes remarks as well: "benevolence can lead to great cruelty… routinely justified by the belief that they are necessary for the prevention of even greater cruelties".[272]

To these voices one can add the celebrated 18th-century penal reformer's, Cesare Beccaria, who, as we read in the third chapter, argued "punishments" to be patently "atrocious", the "public and solemn cruelty" of which could only be lessened by making them "useful… necessary… fair" and consistent with "the goal of the laws". Beccaria did never deny that lawful punishments entail the evil of cruelty. Rather, he argued that, as long as they are rationally grounded in the beneficial spirit of the laws, their painfulness, indeed their declared "cruelty", remains justified.

"Justification" does not annihilate "cruelty", but it makes it better; or, which is *de facto* the same, "unjustified cruelty" is a worse kind of "cruelty".[273] *In nuce* [in essence], there can be such a thing as a lesser evil. Society must protect itself, and the means to achieve this protection, according to Beccaria, can and may involve cruelty, which remains an evil, though necessary or lesser, even if justified. According to Beccaria, the hatred and the fear of crime are sufficient motives to apply cruel measures of prevention and/or correction, in view of the interest of the individual, i.e. "the happiness of this mortal life", and of society as an aggregate thereof: "the greatest happiness for the greatest number".[274] Beccaria opposed "the right [of people]… to slaughter their kin", i.e. the then-commonplace institution of capital punishment, because such extreme forms of punishment harden the souls of citizens, hence nullifying the effect of deterrence that punishments, in his instrumentalist view, should possess.[275] The alternative that he proposed, namely life-long imprisonment, was not selected for its kindness, given that "permanent penal servitude is as grievous as death, and therefore as cruel."[276] As a general rule, prolonged imprisonment was deemed preferable to "tortures" or "executions" upon considerations of utility, insofar as it possesses better chances to deter *via* "the long and sorrowful example of a man deprived of his freedom, who, turned into a beast of burden, pays back the offended society with his services, which is the most powerful impediment to crimes".[277]

In more recent times, John Austin (1911–1960) echoed the British authors quoted above: "A punishment… is an evil: the pain inflicted on the criminal is being added to the mischief of the crime."[278] Not dissimilar is the position of Herbert Lionel Adolphus Hart (1905–1992), who was unusually and candidly explicit in this regard. When defining the "standard or central case of 'punishment,' [he did so] in terms of five elements:"

1. It must involve pain or other consequences normally considered unpleasant.

2. It must occur for an offence against legal rules.

3. It must be of an actual or supposed offender for his offence.

4. It must be intentionally administered by human beings other than the offender.[279]

5. It must be imposed and administered by an authority constituted by a legal system against which the offence is committed.[280]

Clause (i) is essential here, as it makes clear that punishment is in place in order to cause people to suffer.

In spite of this consistent line of agreement on the certain painfulness and likely evil character of lawful punishment, all the aforementioned authors agree upon *not* to abolish the institution of penal justice. None of them is willing to forsake the possibility of sanctioning with duly administered pain those who trespass upon the official laws of the commonwealth. Not even when, as in Beccaria's case, it is acknowledged that the main cause for crime within society is not individual fault, but a faulty economic structure requiring private property, providing the instruments for, and fostering the pursuit of its increase. Society, to them all, whatever systemic injustices it may engender, is quite plainly inconceivable without an awesome, painful power of this kind.

Rare are glimpses of any deeper self-critical insight, such as the one by self-declared retributivist Jeffrie G. Murphy (b. 1940), who recognises that all punishments can be reasonably regarded as "cruel and unusual", hence as unconstitutional according to US law, for: (1) they are meant to produce pain that is "excessive", inasmuch as it could be avoided *tout-court* by employing alternative means; and (2) they are "unusual" because of their practical application, inasmuch as no real legal system whatsoever can ensure that lawful punishment affects only and all those who truly deserve it, i.e. that it is not unfair and partial in its concrete use.[281] Nevertheless, Murphy himself wishes not to subvert the parameters inside which almost all legal theorists operate, i.e. the received view of retributivism, which is commonly opposed to utilitarianism and, together with retributivism, taken as the only genuine options available in jurisprudence. Doing otherwise would mean to join the "extravaganza" of marginal defenders of "treatment" or "forgiveness", which Murphy cannot take seriously *ipso dicto*.[282] According to his analysis, lawful punishments are too entrenched a praxis in social life for us to reject them *in toto*. Consequently, in order not to sound "absurd", he deems it better to distinguish between those punishments that offend our moral sentiments (e.g. "mutilation and torture") and those that do not.[283]

What Murphy and mainstream legal theories do not seem to fully grasp, however, is that it is hardly extravagant that there exist people whose moral sentiments find today's standard lawful punishments repulsive and horrific, not just the gruesome "punishments of bygone days" that Murphy and theorists like him reject (not to mention countries, such as today's Saudi Arabia, where pre-Enlightenment sensitivity and punishments still prevail).[284] People have been disagreeing about what sort of punishments may be acceptable since the earliest days of Roman jurisprudence; one's own private moral sentiments, even if agreeing with one's own publicly esteemed colleagues', are not the only ones that exist in society, and may be even just as relevant as the others. Still, the experts lead the way. The painful evil of penal justice, though amply acknowledged, is not rejected, "extravagant" cases aside. Quite the opposite, it is accepted, if not commended. Depending on the onlooker, order, wealth, the constant reminder of authority, justice, or the promotion of civic virtues are seen as depending upon it. Under this perspective, the divergences between the two major schools in today's theory of punishment, namely those of retribution and deterrence, are not particularly meaningful.[285] Both schools came to life to justify the existing practice of punishment, namely to justify the repression of crime and the exclusion of the criminal from public life. Till the present day, neither school has succeeded in proving itself right once and for all. On the contrary, philosophers and legal theorists have been spending at least three centuries debating this topic, siding with one school or the other, mixing elements of both, no winner having been proclaimed yet.[286] Meanwhile, crime continues to plague societies.

Deviant Criminology

A notable exception is constituted by the Norwegian criminologist Nils Christie (1928–2015), who does perceive and openly condemns the persistence of evil within the painful institution of penal justice and claims that, given the prolonged historical persistence of crime, it may be time to seek other forms of justice altogether. Christie describes himself as a "moral imperialist", i.e. he strongly believes that "pain" is most of the time an "evil" and that, as such, it ought to be reduced to a bare minimum: a "kind world" is, in his view, much preferable to a "painful world".[287] Sometimes, as Christie admits, growing pains can be good; yet, so many significant minds in the history of Western and Eastern cultures and much of one's own personal memories teach us that pain is generally negative. Not to try to reduce pain would be inconsiderate and, ultimately, it would *de facto* legitimise, if not *de iure*, "hell created by man".[288]According to Christie, there is already enough non-man-made (or natural) pain to experience and, infrequently, benefit from; let us not add to it avoidable man-made pain.[289]

Christie accuses criminologists and legal theorists of not being interested in this pain-averse moral attitude or, if interested, of not being consistent with it, which he regards as the only genuinely humane and one that is far better justified than the alternatives, especially in light of the regular failure of penal systems to tackle crime and, above all, its deeper social and psychological roots. In his view, contemporary theory of punishment (aka penal theory) does little or nothing to counteract the presence of avoidable pain. Quite the opposite, it prevents its discussion as a problem by assuming it away *a priori* and, eventually, it fosters its presence by taking the Enlightenment understanding of penal justice for granted, i.e. it reduces the options on the table to utilitarianism, retributivism, or to combinations of the two.[290] Such a commonplace understanding, as Christie assesses it, has rarely touched upon the real depths of the issue of penal evil, i.e. society's fundamental ethical and axiological presuppositions about the nature and functions of pain in human life. Christie argues that, when dealing with the laws that we ought to have in order to promote a better society, we are not arguing merely about institution-specific aspects of social life, such as prisons or gas chambers, but about the change or preservation of the broader system of values that we share. Serious jurisprudence and criminology call for reflection in social philosophy and value theory. Goals and opportunities in life, defining and ascribing blame, choosing desirable forms of governance, seeking social peace or rebellion and much else, are all at stake when tackling the idea that "criminals should suffer"; why are most alleged experts not recognising this simple truth?[291]

According to Nils Christie, the answer to this interrogative resides in the intellectual appeal of what he dubs "neo-classicism", i.e. the 20th-century recovery of the Enlightenment penal mind-set, which in turn finds its roots in the works of several 18th-century 'reformers', Cesare Beccaria's *in primis*.[292] This mind-set, which tries to apply to human affairs the linear causality of Newtonian physics, confounds problem-solving with problem-simplification, and reduces as much as possible all matters of legal responsibility to an actor's episode-specific set of intentions and effects, leaving outside the broader socio-historical context whence emerge both the actor and her legally salient actions. Reality's complexity is conveniently avoided *ab initio* [from the start]. Philosophy and philosophers are not engaged. The roots of the matter are conveniently buried in a "hidden curriculum" that rewards self-censoring experts pursuing "complete clarity, predictability, and pre-programmed behaviour suited for administrative control"; within such a mind-set, "training in law is training in simplification".[293]

In virtue of their economic and political convenience as well as of their formulaic appeal, notions like "deterrence", just retribution and "crime control" maintain their strength in spite of the huge amount of contrary empirical evidence that even classically minded studies have been producing and, at the same time, ignoring for decades.[294] These standard notions are actually professional myths, according to Christie, because the retributivist and utilitarian faith in "crime control" is a mere phantom: penal justice, whether it is exercised in the name of retribution or in that of deterrence, does not control crime.[295] In our Newtonian-physics-inspired cause-and-effect penal systems, most serious crimes go unpunished, and the application of the law remains utterly biased upon factors such as wealth, race and gender.[296] With a pinch of sarcasm, Christie observes that, when dealing with the fairly rare yet most unpalatable crimes, "ritual blame" would be probably as efficient as standard penal justice, and surely less costly for both the State and the taxpayer.[297]

In spite of all the contrary evidence accumulated over the last century, once a form of cruelty has been consecrated institutionally, then its dismissal becomes practically impossible and theoretically counter-intuitive. As John Kenneth Galbraith (1908–2006) once stated, "[c]ommon sense is another term for what has always been believed."[298] Habit generates barriers to recognition, and even the fact that the penal institution relies upon crude "retribution" akin to "revenge" disappears from view.[299] Actual human beings are involved in penal justice, though. Christie argues that we should not neglect the banal point that prisoners are still members of our community that, for the most part, "share most of ordinary people's values."[300] To them, "pain", "deprivation of liberty" and "confinement" are as obnoxious as they would be to any other citizen, and that is what existing penal systems typically deliver.[301] Thus, Christie's writings are meant, first of all, to re-disclose the painful nature of punishment: "The penal system is there to hurt people, not to help or cure. And the pain is inflicted to further the interests of persons other than those brought to suffer."[302]

Given the immediate acceptance of the painful character of actual penal systems, Christie argues that contemporary criminologists, legal theorists and jurists remain locked in the medieval expiatory model that the Enlightenment reformers intended to supersede. Despite repeated claims about 'progress' and 'humaneness', actual penal systems are still based upon retribution and, incessantly, they generate pain. Yet, speaking allegedly in the name of science rather than religion, mainstream 'modern' theorists pretend that somehow, perhaps merely *de iure*, these systems work and do actually combine the virtues of retribution with those of utility by securing social order. Sometimes, they even pretend that utility alone is the justification for penal justice, as ineffective as it is in reality. Academic debates are fought on the terrain of abstract notions and extreme, black-and-white cases, which are as potent in legitimising painful remedies as they are exceptional. By so doing, whilst the gaze is shifted from the messy reality of deviant behaviour and imperfect justice onto far more painless theoretical matters, "legitimacy" is "given to pain" in daily penal praxes.[303]

On a parallel level, a high sense of self-righteousness develops in the administrators of punishment, such that the responsibility for the pain at stake is placed upon the individual who has trespassed upon the social rules, which are assumed *a priori* to be good, and nobody else. No guilt on behalf of those who inflict pain upon others enters the scene, despite the fact that, rather often, this pain is considerable and largely unrelated to whatever proportionality may have been sanctioned in a court of law. In the prisons of the 'civilised' Western world, not to mention those of less affluent countries, phenomena such as overcrowding, rape, inmates' verbal and physical humiliation are the rule, not the exception.[304] We do have a lot of empirical evidence of this dreadful state of affairs, thanks to the research pursued by many criminologists.[305]

Additionally, were we to take scientific investigation seriously, it would become evident that criminal problems are intrinsically, though perhaps not exclusively, social problems, and that many can be resolved at the social level before they shift up to the penal level. Less traumatic forms of intervention are available, which allow for the effective prevention of crime. Man-made pain can be reduced. As the cases of Christie's Norway and of 20th-century Western Europe display, a well-established and richly funded welfare state has proved repeatedly and reliably capable of reducing crime rates. Poor policy is, on the contrary, at the core of the "creation of crime".[306] Old-age pensions, social services, unemployment benefits, training and retraining programmes, healthcare provision and universal education make it possible for huge sectors of the population not to have to rely on crime for their living, hence reducing blue-collar crime. Conversely, their reduction or removal has the opposite effect.[307]

Painful Alternatives

Nils Christie is not a utopian writer. For decades, he was the most famous criminologist in Scandinavia, and his views have been taken into serious account by Norwegian, Swedish and Danish penologists, legislators and journalists for at least thirty years. He knows his enemy—pain—and he does not even deny that there are problems with regard to the alternatives to pain that he himself seeks. For one, society often seems "impotent" *vis-à-vis* crime.[308] Also, crime may hurt "the architects of the welfare state" themselves, who therefore become less "progressive" and find satisfaction in "hurting back" by means of tougher laws.[309] Moreover, there have been many attempts in substituting "punishment" with "treatment", which have proved, at times, unfortunate.[310]

Christie recalls how in Scandinavia, especially after the Second World War, the "progressive" attitude became prevalent and penal policies promoted the medicalisation of criminal problems, many of which were related to alcohol abuse.[311] Therefore, the burden of coping with social disorders and crimes was transferred from penal justice onto public healthcare. The results were encouraging, insofar as many former inmates were now cured and not just punished, thus contributing to their well-being as well as the prevention of future crimes. At the same time, the State's prisons were relieved from hundreds of alcoholics with whom they had to deal daily, and the resources of the State's machinery for "crime control" could be concentrated on the remaining forms of illegality. However, "treatment" was not devoid of flaws.[312] First of all, some people could not be treated. No matter how advanced medical knowledge is, the limitations of human ingenuity and financial resources afflicted and still afflict this scientific field of study.[313] Secondly, "treatment" can turn easily into a new form of "repression", rather than "cure", looking suspiciously like "punishment".[314] Thirdly, the burden from which penal justice had been freed was now on the shoulders of healthcare services, which were not always ready to face the new challenge. Fourthly, horror in the name of social order turned out not to be an exclusive aspect of penal justice: *horribilia* could also take place in hospitals, clinics, dormitories and other healthcare facilities.

The presence of flaws, as disturbing as it may sound, does not imply that we should return to punishment, according to Christie. In general, the means that are employed to treat a criminal are less likely to bring about suffering than those of commonplace lawful punishment. Also, in treatment there is no intrinsic retributive imposition of pain although, as Christie himself remarks, experience teaches that it can occur. Finally, rather than stepping back, one should try to step forward, by identifying new measures that may reduce man-made pain even more.[315]

Christie-an Alternatives

In order to offer his own alternatives to avoidable painful punishment and treatment, Christie envisages social bodies where breaking the rules is usually resolved in non-punitive fashions, such as conciliatory debate between conflicting parties, restitution and forgiveness.[316] Examples of these types of community can be found in ancient rural Scandinavia, post-1968 Danish collectives, and the communities of psychotics gathering in self-administered villages in 1980s Western Norway.[317] In all of these environments, members live mostly on commonly owned resources and five socio-epistemic factors are deemed to play a crucial role among them: "knowledge", "power", "vulnerability", "mutual dependence" and the "belief system" are shared to a very high degree.[318] In these communities, no extreme specialisation or complex division of labour, whether intellectual or manual, has much room, nor is there any significant social stratification and hierarchy. All members are, *grosso modo* [roughly], on an equal footing. No man-made pain, at least as we know it, has any relevant institutional function either; or, if it has any, it is less frequently employed than in today's liberal democracies.[319]

According to Christie, crime should be regarded as a social failure for it to be socially redressed; not as a personal failure in an abstract scheme of things that a neutral, aloof arbiter has to adjudicate upon and, if so reckoned, direct chastisement.[320] For this reason, Christie is considered a prominent herald of *restorative* justice. According to this minor school of thought—which is "minor" if compared to the leading utilitarian and retributive schools—crime is an expression of conflict within the civil community that affects everybody and to which everybody should respond actively as the judge and, if necessary, as the punisher.[321] Though Murphy would perhaps dub it "extravagant" and "absurd", restorative justice has ancient roots and has found many manifestations in non-punitive responses to crime, whether by means of judicial arbitration, reconciliation panels (e.g. South Africa's Truth and Reconciliation Commission of 1995–2000) and so-called "alternative" dispute resolution (e.g. victim-offender mediation, family- or broader-group conferencing, restorative boards). Despite significant achievements, it remains limited in application, as it is used almost exclusively in connection with either nation-wide post-war or post-regime-change contexts, for which standard penal remedies would be highly impractical or improbable, or to small-scale church-, native-tribe-, school- or local-community-based institutions dealing with juvenile and petty delinquency.[322]

Within the egalitarian civil-community contexts explored by Christie, all members know enough about the criminal as a particular person and about the conditions in which the supposed crime emerged. All members have roughly the same power and they know that they could be in the same position as the criminal, whom they are judging, for they are potentially as vulnerable as she is. All members depend upon one another's skills, active work and participation in order to live and keep their community running, at least as much as they depend on their own. All members share a common set of beliefs, in which they trust and which they try actively to bring to fruition. The result of these factors in the equation of justice is that punishment is, according to the statistics available, rare: conciliatory debate, restitution and forgiveness are, instead, predominant.[323] Can these less painful systems be transposed onto the larger, modern, post-industrial Western State?

In Christie's view, they can, albeit incompletely. As he notices, these realities have existed or still exist within mass-scale States. They must be partially compatible with such States, then. Within these larger environments, the alternatives to standard penal praxis represent an ideal goal of reduced pain, which Christie's motto synthesises as follows: "So little State as we dare. So small systems as we dare. So independent systems as we dare. So egalitarian systems as we dare. So vulnerable participants as we dare. In such cases they would be inhibited in using pain."[324] The practical translation of Christie's alternatives into plain bureaucratic terms would be the constitution of small-scale conciliatory boards where all members of the local community (village, neighbourhood, factory, university, etc.) rotate as accusing, defending, judging, and punishing members. Everybody would participate to supply and acquire knowledge in front of the accused person(s), alongside whom she would have to live afterwards *qua* members of the very same community. As Christie insists, we do not need experts for everything, for we do not want to have always sharp separations in knowledge, vulnerability, mutual dependence, and belief. Small-scale bodies, where all citizens may participate, would reduce these critical gaps. Justice would not be gained through a Rawlsian "veil of ignorance", but through knowledge of the context as well as consequences of one's own actions onto specific individuals that we know and with whom we can identify, either as "victims" or as "perpetrators".[325]

On a contrary note, the entire contemporary penal machine has a crude "retributive" element at its very heart, which it expresses through "representation", i.e. abstraction from the concrete person and context and their translation into tokens of abstract ideas.[326] The mediation between "retribution" and its ideological reconstruction, that is, its "representation", creates gaps in knowledge, power, mutual vulnerability, mutual dependence, belief, and, ultimately, it mines actual responsibility and true justice.[327] In Christie's view, the "representative" structure operates through highly technical and Kafkaesque itineraries that obscure the knowledge of what has happened and why and when, etc., whilst at the same time producing very articulate and highly technical pictures of the reality that it supposedly deals with.[328] All powers are bestowed upon this abstract deciding apparatus, so that only one party is vulnerable, for the apparatus itself is independent from the very existence of the particular parties involved in the specific case. This adds remoteness to remoteness in the legal machinery, leaving only a very thin layer of belief and of common purpose in which observers and participants can identify themselves. Christie's fundamental intuition is that, in contrast, a higher sense of responsibility can develop from a condition of reciprocal closeness, which is the exact opposite of what happens in the courts of law today. In the latter environment, legal experts learn to neutralise closeness by acquiring distance from the actual persons involved in the legal case.[329] Christie's conclusion is that, instead, within smaller-scale egalitarian institutions, "listening" can prevail on "force", "compromise" on "dictates", "compensation" on "reprisals" and, "in an old-fashioned language, good on evil."[330]

Christie-an Evil

Christie admits that the various reconciliation boards experimented with in many a State may not be enough to cope with all sorts of crimes. There can be hideous crimes for which the members of the community would still request the harshest punishment and the abstract, hierarchical setting of a more austere court of law. It is also true, however, that the vast majority of known crimes are petty crimes, which could be easily handled by such smaller-scale, more egalitarian boards; but one cannot deny that some crimes do escape from this larger category. Compensation for the offended might well come often through discussion, rather than through a distant expert apparatus for decision-making, but this is not going to be the only case communities are to encounter in their actual existence. Painful punishment, in other words, can be very much reduced and restricted, but it cannot be eliminated altogether, especially as particularly brutal crimes are concerned.[331]

Also, as it was already the case for treatment, the potential for man-made pain resides in restoration too. As there are people that cannot be treated, so there are individuals that cannot be restored or rehabilitated. This may happen because the criminal is incapable of engaging in the beneficial communal structures of reconciliation available to her, but also because there can be "vengeful victims" refusing any sort of compromise.[332] More radically, Christie recognises that his "moral imperialism" implies a paradoxical element, i.e. forgiveness. The paradox of "forgiveness" highlights how the opposition to man-made pain can be cruel to those who perceive themselves as justly endowed with the right to avenge the wrongs suffered, whether this right is to find expression in the form of legal procedures or in that of personal vendetta.[333] Christie admits that there is no easy answer to this paradox, and that his "moral imperialism" is conditional and circularly based upon his own reading of historical and personal experiences.[334] In essence, *if and only if* we want to reduce "pain", then "forgiveness" is going to be more effective than "revenge."[335]

Concluding Remarks

The recognition of the painful evil that is inherent to justified punishment does not require being as chronologically modern or as politically progressive as Nils Christie. The fierce, medieval Dante Alighieri provides a fascinating example in the same direction. Specifically, in his *Divine Comedy*, during his fantastic journey through Hell, Dante encounters the souls of sorcerers and fortune-tellers, who are being punished because of their pagan stupefactions and self-interested deceits. When they were alive, these sorcerers and fortune-tellers twisted the truth, making up wonders and monstrosities that frightened and awed their victims, leading them astray and into sin. Therefore, sorcerers and fortune-tellers are condemned to suffer for all eternity in a way that is to remind them of their own sin, according to the logic of *contrappasso* [lit. counter-step] regulating all infernal punishments. Their heads are now twisted around 180° and their bodies move in a sorrowful, wrong, monstrous fashion:[336]

> *[E] vidi gente per lo vallon tondo*
> *venir, tacendo e lagrimando, al passo*
> *che fanno le letane in questo mondo.*
> *Come 'l viso mi scese in lor più basso,*
> *mirabilmente apparve esser travolto*
> *ciascun tra 'l mento e 'l principio del casso,*
> *ché da le reni era tornato 'l volto,*
> *e in dietro venir li convenia,*
> *perché 'l veder dinanzi era lor tolto...*
> *Se Dio ti lasci, lettor, prender frutto*
> *di tua lezione, or pensa per te stesso*
> *com' io potea tener lo viso asciutto,*
> *quando la nostra imagine di presso*

vidi sì torta, che 'l pianto de li occhi
le natiche bagnava per lo fesso.[337]

Even a sentimentally robust man of the Middle Ages like Dante Alighieri, within his own fiction, cannot but shed tears before the punishment decreed by God Himself, who is by definition the most perfect and most benevolent of beings. For a moment, Dante identifies himself with the damned: they too were human beings once and, in effect, their human souls are now in front of him—terribly distorted and afflicted. Dante feels compassion for these wretched, disfigured sinners. A slow, horrible, humiliating, severe pain, which is wilfully inflicted by God, is displayed before his eyes, which he cannot stop from weeping. Virgil, who is guiding Dante through the realm of the damned, reproaches him for this incident of untoward humaneness:

Certo io piangea, poggiato a un de' rocchi
   del duro scoglio, sì che la mia scorta
   mi disse: «Ancor se' tu de li altri sciocchi?
Qui vive la pietà quand' è ben morta;
   chi è più scellerato che colui
   che al giudicio divin passion comporta?[338]

In Hell, compassion may not have place. Pity is dead: "divine revenge" is at work.[339] Those who betrayed God are now paying for their culpable foolishness and wrong-headedness: justice is being carried out. If Dante were only less human and more angelic, he would not cry. Instead, he would join God and the Saints, who, as Dante is to realise in *Paradiso*, take delight in seeing the wretched sinners being chastised, for their chastisements are: (1) useful reminders for the living (and the penitent) of that which is right and wrong;[340] (2) necessary counterparts to the eternal life of bliss awaiting the pious believers;[341] and (3) instances of the beautiful, symmetrical order that encompasses God's Creation.[342]

The largely Thomist theory of punishment that pervades Dante's vision of the afterlife possesses a crucial aesthetic element. Not only is it a theory of retributive justice, according to which it is inscribed within the grammar of the universe that evil deeds are to be punished. It is also a theory of retributive beauty, requiring that the perfection of God's Creation should imply the horrible sights before which Dante himself cries. Cruelty is itself a component of the supreme "beauty" embodied by "the horrible art of justice".[343] Dante's inner conflict between the human and the angelic sides could not be expressed more powerfully. No matter how blasphemous Dante's reaction could appear to his contemporaries (as it cast doubt upon God's absolute goodness), he recognised the painful evil inherent to divine punishment.

The sphere of the human (hence humane) and the sphere of the angelic or superhuman (i.e. non-human or even in-humane) do not coexist without trouble, at least as human understanding is concerned. In canto XX of the *Inferno*, Dante is lost between these two poles, as cruelty shows its revolting face to Dante's Christian heart, which nurtures the values of unrestrained mercy and immediate sympathy. At the same time, through Virgil's words, it also shows its logical face to Dante's Christian mind, which appreciates God's symmetry of justice, i.e. the necessary and iron-law-like connection between each person's sins and her chastisement. On the one hand lies the *horribile visu* of cruelty; on the other hand, its cold beauty, i.e. its fitting neatly within the moral cosmic order of God's Creation. Dante, who waves between the two directions, recognises the painful evil of punishment, and redeems it as an instrument in the hands of God's justice, but not without a blatant acknowledgment of its terrible character. Paraphrasing Beccaria, divine norms seem to involve punishments that are "useful... necessary... fair" and consistent with "the goal of the laws" of the God of Life, but the cruelty of which is not denied.

The order and the righteousness of expiation in the medieval Dante and the Enlightenment reformer Beccaria follow lines that, as Christie noticed, have been applied in the modern, reformed and allegedly enlightened centuries too. Dante's retributivism is not equivalent to Beccaria's utilitarian approach: the goal of the laws, the laws themselves and the maker of the laws are different. Yet, there is continuity between these two schools of thought with respect to their acceptance of the evil pains of punishment. If today's Western world is really as secular as it is normally claimed to be, however, then it may be time to make the ruling logic of its penal system less retributivist, less coldly calculating and, perhaps, more conciliatory and forgiving: that is Christie's central claim. Or at least, if such a change is not deemed desirable or opportune, its inherent painfulness and likely evil character ought not to be taken lightly and endorsed uncritically in penal practice and penal theory. We should at least be as brave as Dante and acknowledge the *horribile visu* that we believe to be justified, or that we tacitly legitimise by assuming it as such.

PART III – *LIBERA NOS A CRUDELITATE*

Chapter 7: Disciplinary Divisions and Petty Academics. In Memory of Richard Rorty (1931–2007)

The death of Richard Rorty leaves today's intellectual world without one of its protagonists. Widely read, translated, cited and interviewed, Rorty embodied for the past twenty years a remarkable example of *popular intellectual,* analogous to Bertrand Russell (1872–1970) and Jean-Paul Sartre (1905–1980) in previous decades. It is not clear whether Rorty's popularity was due to the genuine attempt on his part to emulate his illustrious predecessors, or was rather the involuntary result of the ostracism that he suffered from the American philosophical community. Eventually, vexed by the unfriendliness of colleagues that refused to consider him 'one of them', Rorty had even changed his professional affiliation, stepping outside academic philosophy and into the humanities, whilst describing himself as an expert in "social criticism".[344] On their part, professional philosophers, mainly in his native country, had been criticising him since the 1980s as 'vague' and 'non-philosophical', because of his refusal to adhere to the highly technical jargon and selective choice of topics characterising the predominantly analytic academe. Rorty had toyed with such jargon and topics for years, abandoning them later as inadequate *vis-à-vis* the existential, ethical and political issues that he thought befitting relevant philosophical activity, possibly with the sole exception of John Rawls (1921–2002), i.e. another committed US liberal within analytical academia. Like Karl Jaspers (1883–1969) before him, Rorty had come to realise that much of the philosophy practiced in the universities was gratuitously byzantine and spiritually sterile.

Standards

Rorty even theorised an opposition between "relevance" and "rigour", whereby any honest intellectual must accept a certain degree of vagueness, if she wishes to deal with truly important matters and reach the hearts, and not just the minds, of her audience

—possibly a larger one than the mere circle of professional academics.[345] As Chaïm Perelman (1912–1984) had been repeating with limited success before Rorty himself, the wise edifying rhetoric of Aristotle and Giambattista Vico (1668–1744)—not the unwise self-serving one of Gorgias of Leontini (485–380 BC) and Newt Gingrich (b. 1943)—had to be rediscovered by philosophers and by scholars in general. An excessive emphasis on rigour, they concurred, makes the intellectual's endeavour likely to turn into an ivory-tower enterprise. Rorty's approach is reminiscent of the medieval grammarians of Chartres, who, in the name of Christian *charitas* [love, charitableness], opposed (in vain, it must be said) the infatuation of the young universities of Europe with logic and knockout dialectic. Indeed, Rorty, an ethnocentric atheist and a theorist of post-religious society, was never ashamed of admitting that his commitment to political liberalism as a tool for reducing cruelty in the public sphere was contiguous to the long-standing Christian tradition of universal social solidarity and humane, ecumenical acceptance of diversity.

Ecumenical is also Rorty's thought under another important respect, since it embraces influences and contributions from very diverse fields. Rorty's works are the 'home' for a surprisingly rich array of references, including Isaac Newton (1642–1727) and Vladimir Nabokov, Clifford Geertz (1926–2006) and George Orwell, Martin Heidegger and Ian Hacking (b. 1936), Michel Foucault and Willard van Orman Quine (1908–2000), Sigmund Freud (1856–1939) and Umberto Eco (1932–2016). True to his pragmatist inspirers, Rorty believed all disciplines to be nothing but attempts of the human being to face, and hopefully resolve, difficulties arisen in our environment. There is nothing essentially different between history, physics, psychoanalysis, or astrology. Disciplinary divisions are super-imposed, sometimes for pragmatic reasons, other times for political reasons, occasionally for moral reasons. This is done, *inter alia* [among other things], in order to separate and prioritise those difficulties that we wish seen resolved, serve the interests of a ruling group, or praise those researchers that we admire as examples of integrity.

Rorty became quickly as controversial as he was increasingly popular, and the ostracism encountered amidst American philosophers pushed him beyond the boundaries of professional philosophy and beyond the boundaries of his native country. His prose became progressively more and more accessible, richer in anecdotes and witticisms, and less and less identifiable within a single disciplinary field. His works started targeting, and appealing to, non-philosophers, attaining popularity amongst academics and non-academics interested in the humanities, in politics and in the social sciences. In particular, he was received with warmth and sincere curiosity in Continental Europe, especially in Italy and France, where being interdisciplinary and able to reach the general public are considered to be virtues, at least, if not requirements for philosophers dealing with socio-political issues. Continuing the experience of the Enlightenment, *filosofi* and *philosophes* are expected there to take part in the ongoing political debates of their countries. Moreover, Rorty's neo-pragmatism echoed in several ways Gianni Vattimo's (b. 1936) *pensiero debole* [weak thought] and Jean-François Lyotard's (1924–1998) postmodernism; with the benefit of hindsight, its reception in the Old World was not overly difficult to achieve.

Under several important respects, Rorty belongs in spirit and aims to the same family of Western minds as Sextus Empiricus (160–210 AD), Erasmus of Rotterdam (1466–1536), Michel de Montaigne, Voltaire and George Santayana (1863–1952). These all are thinkers who, in different times and in different guises, challenged the dogmas of received wisdom, yet avoiding at the same time any sceptical or aestheticist indifference to the human suffering surrounding them. They all attempted to develop pragmatic and life-sensitive responses to the many sorrows of the actual human being, whilst resisting the temptation of turning philosophy into elitist escapism or abstract justification of the status quo, its injustices, its painful habits and praxes, and its ruling elites. The sufferings of humans and, sometimes, of other living creatures too, were their focus point and their paramount concern, not the quest for certainty, scrupulous demonstration, or victory in argument, even when conducive to academic career and economic status. Unsurprisingly, they all are commonly recalled as *humanists*, for they posited the human condition at the centre of their thought.

Encounters

I encountered the work of Richard Rorty in Genoa, Italy, as a young philosophy student. In those days, I was trying to come to terms with the 'fathers' of post-analytic philosophy (e.g. Quine) in an academic setting, the Italian universities of the early 1990s, where the analytic tradition was yet to establish itself firmly. Then, the 'daring' students and some of the younger teachers of the Faculty of Letters and Philosophy formed a group attracted by the fairly 'new' and 'trendy' analytic philosophy and, by extension, the even 'newer' and 'trendier' post-analytic offshoots. Clear amidst them was the stylish appeal of 'hard-core' formulae, of linguistic hair-splitting as proof of acumen, and of the intriguing ramifications in the English-speaking fields of artificial intelligence, mathematical logic, cognitive science and select areas of biology. The more 'traditional' group of students preferred instead the well-established teachings of ancient, medieval and modern philosophy, which led often to the exploration of German- and French- speaking 'classics', whether old or recent. My interests covered both areas, cutting across both groups of students and mentors. Yet, as I am about to explain, Rorty made me opt for the former, albeit in a somewhat indirect manner.

I encountered Richard Rorty in person, once again in Italy. It was the summer of 1997 and I had the opportunity to indulge with him in a long, pleasant day of conversation on all sorts of topics at the Rockefeller Foundation of Villa Serbelloni in Bellagio, on the Como Lake. Rorty was remarkably more modest and composed than I expected. After reading his written work, full of wit and drama, I had formed in my mind the picture of a complacent and histrionic man of great intellectual power, prone to sharp gibes and excited story-telling. Instead, his tone was calm and demure, almost monotonous, his humour was infrequent and inessential to the discussed topics, his speech slow, articulate and careful in elucidating the reasons *pro* and *contra* whichever thesis we were debating. His mind was unmistakably and robustly analytic, although his evident yet unpretentious erudition allowed him to be gloriously synthetic as well, painting cultural shifts and historical sketches with few effective strokes. In the meanwhile, the sun kept shining in the sky, sometimes pleasantly, other times mercilessly, as customary of Italian summers, its hot light revealing the architectural beauty of the patrician mansion that hosted us. We dined together *al fresco* [outdoors], carrying the conversation further, while enjoying the kind company of Rorty's wife and of other guests of the Foundation. Dusk approached, yet the temperature remained sufficiently warm to allow the chilled white wine served at the table to be a perfect companion to the discussion. Unfortunately, the chef was not a native of the area—I recall him as a young man from the East Coast of the United States of America—and the meal prepared did not seem to take full advantage of the local produce. Actually, it looked nice but had hardly any taste. My surprise and disappointment in that respect are still vivid in my memory: why would well-off Americans, hosts of the Rockefeller Foundation, be in Italy and eat poorly?

Apart from resulting in an interview published by the journal *Iride* of the Gramsci Institute of Florence, that striking day in Bellagio proved decisive in determining the topic of my laureate thesis, which I devoted entirely to Rorty's thought and defended the following year at the University of Genoa. Specifically, I concentrated on how Rorty's criticism of Western "representationalism" was logically and ethically intertwined with his defence of political liberalism. In order to do this, I had to familiarise myself further with the analytic tradition, which he reproached so forcefully—and this is how Rorty made me opt for the analytic group in an indirect manner. After completing my studies in Italy, I kept in touch with Rorty by e-mail, fine-tuning the text of the interview to be published. Also, I was considering the possibility of studying with him at the University of Virginia, if ever accepted in their graduate programme, which happened in the year 1999. In the meanwhile, however, Rorty had decided to move to Stanford and I, left without the desired mentor there, opted for another destination, i.e. the University of Guelph, in Canada. Better funding, direct admission into the doctoral programme, my 'hero' John Kenneth Galbraith having studied there, and the fact that they had contacted me by phone in order to convince me to join them told me that I would have fared better in Ontario than in Virginia. I spent three years in Guelph, the time needed to obtain a PhD title.

My sojourn in that vast and beautiful country was a most revealing experience, which helped me to understand as well the rather bizarre climate of philosophy departments on the other side of the Atlantic Ocean and the sort of unpleasantness that must have plagued Rorty's professional life to the point of making him change expert affiliation. The divide between analytic and so-called "Continental" philosophy had never been a real issue while I studied in Italy, perhaps because of the limited self-assertion of the former back then, or simply because of the lack of meaning of the term "Continental" on the Continent, where more significant distinctions are drawn by reference to specific schools and traditions (e.g. phenomenology, Thomism, existentialism) or to the language in which philosophers write (e.g. Latin, French, Russian). Things were different in Canada and, as I was soon to ascertain by way of conferences and conversations, in the United States of America too. There, the divide between analytic and Continental philosophy meant a great deal to a good number of people: belonging to a faction; knowing whom to side with on committees and other internal academic bodies; realising whom to snare at or dismiss as intellectually naïve and aimless; keeping lists of friends and foes; spotting and co-opting good students before the perceived adversary did the same. The philosophy department at Guelph was not even a particularly bad case. Most of the time, the philosophers working there forgot about factions and allegiances, cooperating wonderfully within a rich, diverse, stimulating array of courses and activities. Harmony was not at all a rarity, but it lasted until the time for hiring new staff came about. Then, as though someone had unleashed their angry spirits, they started clubbing verbally at one another, exchanging nasty e-mails, and spreading rumours against their supposed enemies. The young philosophers seemed more rabid than the older ones, probably due to higher levels of testosterone in their body or to the need for approval by the older colleagues, who retain the terrifying power to turn tenure into an unattainable dream. There were exceptions, though, namely philosophers who regarded themselves as mere philosophers: curious minds exploring rationally anything that stimulated their interest. Still, they were exceptions and, as such, they resulted odd or suspicious. Not knowing which faction to join, and taking both analytic and 'Continental' courses, I ended up working with one of these exceptions, a brilliant Marxist scholar in the process of becoming Canada's 'green' *maître à penser* [thinker of reference, leading mind].

At the same time, I had several opportunities to discuss and write about Rorty, whose thought had penetrated deep within my perception of reality, philosophical as well as non-philosophical. Almost immediately, I realised that he was not welcome. Predictably, the analytic philosophers disliked him openly and deeply, for Rorty in his writings kept telling them that they, quite frankly, were wasting their time in futile hyper-technical squabbles. Less predictably, the Continental ones disliked him too. Why this was the case is not yet fully clear to me. Perhaps Rorty had simply been too successful; and success breeds envy, which is then rationalised into critical argument. Perhaps he could not be pigeon-holed to their satisfaction; as a re-discoverer of the one and only truly American philosophical school and self-proclaimed "neo-pragmatist", Rorty could not be enlisted in their 'army', which was Continental by definition. Whatever the reason, I was encouraged in making my essays about him more critical than they tended to be in their first draft, where I usually acknowledged the value of Rorty's contribution to whichever relevant topic I was exploring and assessing. Analogous advice I received from blind referees commenting on papers submitted for publication to professional journals. Overall, a streak or fashion of 'anti-Rortyanism' was sweeping across Anglophone philosophers.

I do not intend to deny that there are good reasons to disagree with Rorty on a number of issues. I have written a good deal on aspects of his thought that I found unconvincing or even contradictory, as the following chapters also show. Still, what I wish to point out is that I encountered an opposition to his thought that resembled more resentment than disagreement, thus obliterating or at least underplaying the many noteworthy teachings that can be drawn from his intellectual production. Therefore, I wish to conclude by highlighting and applying something that can be learnt from Rorty, namely the interconnectedness of all disciplines on genealogical, practical and moral grounds.

Definitions

Although never contrary to disciplinary divisions as temporary arrangements for organising the training and the application of the human genius, Rorty denounced the repeated historical attempts to set hierarchies amidst the disciplines and prioritise one for its special ability to tell us what the world is *really* like (e.g. theology, philosophy, poetry, physics). All disciplines are only, in his view, *instruments*, which we use when trying to cope with the environment surrounding us. Moreover, Rorty was perplexed by the way in which academic bureaucracy created further artificial divisions amongst disciplines that share much ground, thus contributing to the fragmentation of the enterprise called "human knowledge" *via* the systemic entrenchment of professorial fiefdoms, self-serving titles, politically motivated preferential funding and assorted ransoms.

For the past several years, I have been teaching at my university in Iceland history of ideas, critical thinking, contemporary history, pedagogy, penal theory and ethics across three or four faculties, the main one being the Faculty of Law and Social Sciences (now called of "Humanities and Social Sciences"): two faculties in one by itself, hence my uncertainty about their number. Regularly, I have met many students telling me that, to their surprise, they had realised that several issues debated in their favourite field of study, whether biology, anthropology or constitutional law, had already been and/or were still discussed by seemingly passé 'unscientific' philosophers and theologians. Not to mention the numerous times when they had been required to study the work of philosophers and theologians *tout-court*, whether Aquinas and Thomas Hobbes in jurisprudence, Auguste Comte (1798–1857) and Karl Marx (1818–1883) in sociology, or William James (1842–1910) and Rollo May (1909–1994) in psychology. As unavoidable and disturbing as this experience may have been, they had discovered something very important, i.e. that the existing disciplinary boundaries were less precise than academic bureaucracy, widespread social consciousness, and governmental policy had led them to assume before commencing their university studies. Rorty would have been proud of these students, whose intelligence had not been stifled entirely by received views, educated prejudice and repeated disjunction of disciplinary terms in official curricula (e.g. human vs. social sciences, humanities vs. sciences, arts vs. sciences, hard vs. soft sciences, natural vs. human sciences, philosophy vs. social sciences), each of which periodically blinds those students' instructors, administrators and decision-making politicians.

Let us examine more closely "philosophy" and "social sciences", for instance. Can there be any tenable essential distinction between them? A *caveat* [warning] is required before answering this question: I am not going to develop an extensive, finely referenced argument. This chapter is in fact built upon an obituary *in memoriam* [commemorating] of Rorty. Henceforth, I wish to share with the readers few 'Rorty-esque' considerations, in order to acknowledge explicitly, at last, that Rorty could be marvellously spot-on.

We can then start with the etymology of the term "philosophy", namely the combination of: (1) the Greek *philein*, i.e. to love (*philia* referring especially to brotherly love and friendship) or to have an interest in (consider contemporary English words like "bibliophile", "philanthropy"; and (2) "hydrophilic"), and *sophia*, i.e. knowledge (especially of the 'disinterested' type) or wisdom. The two following standard definitions should therefore sound uncontroversial: (A) *love of knowledge*; (B) *love of wisdom*. The relevance of this love for knowledge or wisdom is further revealed by the Latin etymology of "study", i.e. *studium*, meaning passion, keenness or fondness. The amateur, for example, is the person who is moved towards certain instances of knowledge or wisdom by genuine *amor* i.e. love. Contemporary Italian translates "amateur" into *dilettante*, i.e. she who amuses herself, which was the term used by Leonardo da Vinci (1452–1512) to describe himself. Professionals, on the contrary, seem to be moved toward the same goal also, if not exclusively, by something else, e.g. greed, fear, habit, duty, peer pressure, lack of alternatives, vanity, will to power, necessity.

Another possibility to define philosophy is by trying to capture the meaning of expressions such as "what is your philosophy?", or "the philosophy of our institution / association / company is…". In this case, we can arguably infer that "philosophy" means: (C) *expressing the ultimate rationale(s) of a given entity*; (D) *expressing the ultimate value(s) of a given entity.* Alternative renderings are possible, but let us work with these four hypotheses and move on to the definition of social science. The encyclopaedia most commonly cited by my students, the 'infamous' *Wikipedia*, states: (E) *the group of academic disciplines that study the human aspects of the world.* Believe it or not, the definitions available in 'respectable' encyclopaedias do not differ much (e.g. *Encyclopaedia Britannica*: "any discipline or branch of science that deals with human behaviour in its social and cultural aspects").

Given definitions A and E, then the social sciences are nothing but a branch of philosophy, inasmuch as the social sciences are possible by loving, or having an interest in, a certain type of knowledge. In effect, *mutatis mutandis* [changing what needs changed] the whole scientific enterprise falls under the same umbrella. This conclusion should not surprise us, for physics, chemistry and biology were called, at least until the early 19th century, "natural philosophy", as they constituted examples of philosophical inquiry in the realm of particular natural phenomena (and not of super- and sub-natural phenomena, or nature in general). "Natural sciences" has subsequently become the most common label for the same disciplines, although as recently as 1963, the physicist Clifford Ambrose Truesdell (1919–2000) founded the *Society for Natural Philosophy* at the Johns Hopkins University in Baltimore. In addition, from a historical perspective, most sciences, and *all* the social sciences, have developed within the rich fold of activities called "philosophy". Eventually, they have crystallised into the disciplines with which we are now familiar, yet not because of the abandonment of the original love of knowledge, but mainly because of the constitution of modern universities, the consequent division of intellectual labour amongst professional researchers, and the resulting rigid distinction of specific disciplines, which in today's universities go from theoretical physics to business studies, management studies and accounting. The modern 'academisation' of knowledge has progressively introduced stiffer and stiffer boundaries, criss-crossing the 'universe' of knowledge to which 'universities' should be dedicated. The same process has generated the modern expert or specialist, who often knows very little of what goes on outside her narrow area of investigation. In so doing, universities have made the existence of the *dilettante à la* [like] Leonardo not only a rarity, but something unreliable and perplexing, because inconsistent with the official 'pigeon-holes' reified during the 19th and 20th century.

Leonardo da Vinci and René Descartes (1596–1650) would struggle to get an academic position in any of today's major universities. Although original and well-meaning, they would lack the required professional credentials. Analogously, the *Book of Tao* by Lao-Tzu (6th c. BC), Lucretius' (94–50 BC) *De rerum natura* and Galileo's (1564–1642) *Dialogo sui massimi sistemi* would be unlikely to be published as scientific works, for alien to the 'pigeon-holes' of today's scholarship. It must be said that, at least in part, this process of 'academisation' was unavoidable, because of the complexity of certain types of research, requiring years of arduous training to be pursued effectively. In part, however, it was also due to the promotion of disciplinary boundaries as structures of power, e.g. claims to expertise, academic titles, career prospects, scholarly reputation, public recognition, hefty contracts, self-definition and definition of others. One of the last *dilettanti* of the Western world, Arthur Schopenhauer, wrote in 1851 a long essay about and against this process (*Über die Universitäts-Philosophie*), which he judged detrimental to the interdisciplinary cross-fertilisation required for true genius to blossom.[346] This work of his has never been a best-seller amongst professional academics.

Given definitions C and/or D and E, philosophy becomes one of the social sciences, if and insofar as it pursues the study of the human aspects of the world. In particular, philosophers who study objectively (i.e. whose conclusions are accepted inter-subjectively as plausible descriptions and/or explanations of phenomena) and rigorously (i.e. who follow the rules of logic and concurred methods of rational investigation) human phenomena in the attempt to determine their ultimate rationale and/or value, are social scientists. Ethicists, political philosophers, philosophers of the mind and of language clearly fall in this category of researchers. Even when focussing upon normative issues, these philosophers observe, describe and use empirical evidence to assess their hypotheses, adhering to the rules of logic and to agreed methodologies for inquiry, some of which are amongst the oldest and longest-tested in our culture (e.g. Socrates' dialogical method). I mention the notions of objectivity and rigour, since they constitute the two defining criteria employed by Italian philosopher, physicist and mathematician Evandro Agazzi (b. 1934).[347]

According to Agazzi, these criteria allow us to distinguish between reasoned cognitive endeavour and potentially unreasoned cognitive endeavour, whilst still being as open as necessary to avoid the paradoxes arising from stricter definitions. For example, definitions placing emphasis on positive observation, description and cataloguing leave out the creative genius of scientific innovation, i.e. science at its best; definitions placing emphasis on induction or experimentation leave out logic and mathematics, i.e. two fundamental instruments of scientific research; definitions placing emphasis on uniformity of method leave out the actual practice of science in the world's laboratories, i.e. what scientists do, which is not always methodical; and definitions placing emphasis on predictive ability leave out numerous descriptive disciplines, sub-disciplines and important stages in scientific research.

Agazzi's approach is not animated by the desire to expunge certain disciplines from the fold of science, which is something that 'hard' scientists may be prone to do *vis-à-vis*, amongst others, 'soft' scientists, despite the efforts by these 'softies' to mimic physics and chemistry by using formulae and statistical computations in their research, even when unnecessary. In response to 'hard' scientists, 'soft' scientists could then side with the 18th-century Neapolitan polymath Giambattista Vico and argue that only the formal and social sciences (which in his case would be today's humanities) can be actual science, not physics, chemistry and biology. This is the case, according to Vico, because the formal and social sciences deal with creations of the human spirit, hence phenomena whose reasons and/or motives for being the way they are can be determined with enough confidence by the human inquirer. Instead, when it comes to the phenomena studied, say, by the physicist, we may be able to say *how* they work, but not *why*. God alone, if one exists, knows why quarks or hamsters are part of creation.

We might be tempted to integrate the definition *E* by adding that 'actual' sciences employ certain specific methods of investigation, especially mathematical, quantitative or statistical ones. This may sound like a plausible integration, which should strengthen the 'scientificity' of one's discipline, as though such methods were the essence of science itself. Yet, it must be taken *cum grano salis* [with a pinch of salt], if not more than just a grain. First of all, these methods have changed through time, hence one should modify the qualified definition whenever the methods change—what an inconvenience. Secondly, these methods are not followed by all 'actual' scientists under all circumstances. Nobel Prize physicist Percy W. Bridgman (1882–1961) once stated: "No working scientist, when he plans an experiment in the laboratory, asks himself whether he is being properly scientific, nor is he interested in whatever method he may be using *as method.*"[348] Thirdly, these methods have been used, amongst others, by philosophers and have often developed within philosophy (e.g. analysis and infinitesimal calculus). They may not be the most common tools of their trade today, but they are not unknown either and can still spur theoretical insights (e.g. Deleuze, Agazzi). Finally, both 'hard' and 'soft' scientists seem often to forget the very 'soft' elements that are

132

present in each scientific discipline, e.g. creative genius, the deductive elements of inductive science (e.g. mathematical theorems, the *a priori* determination of the sub-atomic particles to be studied experimentally), the inductive elements of deductive science (e.g. the material origin, expression and reviewing of mathematical theorems), the assumed absolute validity of pseudo-absolute stipulations (e.g. our units of measurement of space, time, mass, etc.), and the tacit faith in the existence of truth, material and/or immaterial beings, mutual understanding, and their continuity in time.

Given definitions B and E, the social sciences are philosophy if and insofar as wisdom animates them, whilst they depart from each other whenever wisdom is absent from the former. Unlike the amateur, the professional seem capable of pursuing knowledge without love. Whether they and not the amateur or *dilettante* may thus reach wisdom is an interesting question, for it leads us to consider the difference between knowledge and wisdom. A knowledgeable person, indeed even an accomplished specialist, is not necessarily a wise person. Think only of all the accomplished engineers and physicists who, for money or for nationalism, have contributed to developing the most formidable weapons of mass destruction. Being as knowledgeable as a rocket scientist may not prevent one from being an egregious mass murderer.

What makes us wise, then? Let us reply, for the sake of brevity, with a reference to the teachings of Icelandic philosopher Páll Skúlason (1945–2015), who claims that wisdom consists in a blend of three fundamental ingredients: knowledge, moral integrity, and life experience.[349] It follows from this triad that youth is likely to be unwise and, more importantly, that there cannot be wisdom without knowledge, whilst there can be plenty of knowledge without wisdom. If Páll Skúlason is correct in his understanding of wisdom, then we must assess whether individual researchers are enriching their knowledge of human affairs (i.e. 'mere' social science) with moral integrity *and* life experience. In fact, in order for wisdom to be absent from the social sciences, hence disqualifying them as philosophy, it is the person, not the discipline, that counts.

Concluding Remarks

This consideration about actual persons is commonly exemplified by scientists and researchers that have 'sold themselves', or that are pursuing 'maverick science', or that 'have no shame' and 'no morals'. Intellectual inquirers that bully, cheat, lie, manipulate, prevaricate, scheme, and are generally immoral on the workplace, can therefore belong to the family of social scientists, but not to that of philosophers (which does not imply that so-called "philosophers" be always true philosophers, i.e. lovers of wisdom). In this perspective, the widespread tendency of 'hard' and 'soft' scientists to disqualify each other and, jointly, to kick out of the scientific pantheon those whom they dislike, e.g. humanists or jurists, looks very suspicious. If we consider the etymology of the term "science", after all, it would be plain silly to take sides: "science" derives from the Latin verb *scire*, i.e. to know by means of study and/or meditation. Whether this knowledge is then 'hard' or 'soft' adds little to the fact that it is knowledge. "Hard" and "soft" are much more relevant terms when talking of nougat, mattresses and male sexual organs.

Do not take this remark about male sexual organs as a vulgar joke. As rude as it may sound, it is common English parlance to name "cocky" the supercilious and "pricks" or "dickheads" those who bully others into exclusion. Perhaps, listening to common parlance on this matter may prove the most insightful way to be followed when trying to understand why some scientists and researchers may wish to expunge fellow scientists and researchers from the pristine, supreme and better-funded disciplinary precinct that they long to see established or to maintain undisturbed. Rorty's own lived example of academic ostracism and, above all, his professional choice to focus upon the plight of human beings as living people, in their ordinary environment and with their far-too-familiar sorrows and problems, would support such an openness to common parlance.

Chapter 8: The Ironic and Painful Cornering of Liberalism of Fear

We read in chapter 4 that, according to Richard Rorty, "there is no answer to the question 'Why not be cruel?' – no noncircular theoretical backup for the belief that cruelty is horrible"; in his view, "[a]nybody who thinks that there are well-grounded theoretical answers to this sort of question – algorithms for resolving moral dilemmas of this sort – is still, in his heart, a theologian or a metaphysician... [And a] postmetaphysical culture seems to me no more impossible than a postreligious one, and equally desirable."[350] This passage exemplifies why Rorty is widely held to be a controversial author. How not to experience a sense of loss, disappointment, if not even outrage, when presented with such a manifest desire for what he calls "a postmetaphysical culture"? How not to fear the dramatic frailty of an intellectual world emptied of the chance, if not of the *conatus* [longing] itself, towards the investigation of what is true, rationally compelling, and universally fundamental, which by itself involves the assumption that such a truth, whether ultimately discoverable or not, may at least exist?

We read as well in chapters 1 and 3 that the crucial political and ethical dimensions of Rorty's philosophy, *per* his 1989 book *Contingency, Irony and Solidarity*, purport that "cruelty is horrible" and that "liberals are the people who think that cruelty is the worst thing we do". Rorty declares and portrays himself as a liberal, and devotes most of his intellectual efforts to the promotion of liberal policies. He even dedicates *Contingency, Irony, and Solidarity* "[to the] memory of six liberals: my parents and grandparents."[351] Rorty writes repeatedly that cruelty is bad, but he denies that we can say why it is so once and for all: *we* say that it is so; and that is all that he thinks we can say. Rorty's publications and speeches against all forms of barbarism are replete with anti-metaphysical claims of this ilk.[352] However, how can Rorty advance any sensible objection against cruelty without a fundamental ethical footing of some sort? Can he really claim that he defends liberalism and, at the same time, rely on no metaphysical assumption whatsoever? I sense the presence of a contradiction, possibly *formal* and surely *performative*, as Rorty claims: [A] "No well-grounded theoretical answer" can be given in reply to the interrogative "why not be cruel?"; and [B] "Cruelty is the worst thing we do." The following paragraphs articulate and explain what I sense.

Specifically, this chapter illustrates how a *universal normative ground* lies beneath Rorty's own ethical and political position i.e. a *foundational moral assumption* backing [B], upon which Rorty relies in spite of [A]. In order to do so, I delineate very briefly Rorty's two crucial notions of "ethnocentrism" and "antirepresentationalism" that, together, motivate [A]. With reference to the former notion, I provide a few examples of Rorty's ethical and political beliefs, with the aim of demonstrating that his commitment in favour of political liberalism is not extemporary or superficial. Showing the relevance of liberalism within Rorty's intellectual enterprise is of help in order to highlight the inherent contradiction between [A] and [B], for problematic echoes of this discrepancy are to become evident both with regard to his "ethnocentrism" and with regard to his "antirepresentationalism". Brief critical considerations on both concepts are sketched thereafter, thus providing the reader with a broader spectrum of the flaws that I envisage in Rorty's political project. Subsequently, I focus my attention on [B], i.e. Rorty's conception of liberalism with respect to the issue of *cruelty*. By doing so, I try to determine the essential features of this notion, the study of which contributes to the individuation of the concepts working as the universal normative ground for his liberalism. I am going to argue that Rorty's ethical and political concerns are based on an unexplained *pain-aversion principle*, which regularly supports Rorty's claims against cruelty—and *ergo* [therefore] his claims in favour of liberalism (note that I use here "founding" and "grounding" as synonyms).

Ethnocentrism

Rorty's "ethnocentrism" expresses his refusal of any allegedly rational attempt to provide all humans with *the definitive reasons* whereby certain actions should not be performed, as if they were derivable from the neutral, rational scrutiny of the human condition at any time and in any place. Rorty does not deny that *some reasons* may be provided, but he stresses the point that they are not the necessary, universal, and only reasons that may be given. They are merely those reasons that can succeed within a certain social and temporal context, in which some moral convictions have been enforced by the peculiar conditioning that mythology, literature, politics, law, religion and education have been moulding in a people's culture and in the psyche of the individuals belonging to it. The opposition towards certain behaviours—commonly labelled "evil"—and the favour towards others—labelled "good"—are just a matter of background, mentality, shared sensitivity and sensibility. One's own *Bildung* [upbringing, education, formation] determines one's own rationality and, *a fortiori*, one's own ethics and one's own politics.

Philosophers are not the discoverers of the unshakable, profound foundations of ethics and politics. For Rorty, they cannot do much else but remind their fellows of what is evil and good within their historical, social context:

> *Moral principles (the categorical imperative, the utilitarian principle, etc.) only have a point insofar as they incorporate tacit reference to a whole range of institutions, practices, and vocabularies of moral and political deliberation. They are reminders of, abbreviations for, such practices, not justifications for such practices. At best, they are pedagogical aids to the acquisition of such practices.* [353]

All that guides human action in creating political projects, all that forces humans to abide to certain patterns of action, is their grip on a deep contingent cluster of moral intuitions that are shared locally.

Any attempt to provide a universal and definitive justification of any set of values cannot avoid circularity, since it will eventually rest on these values themselves as decisive presuppositions. One's own moral or political intuitions are not a leap into the realm of truth, nor are they a deduction obtained from such a realm; intuitions are just a matter of socially and historically determined paradigms of rationality, accepted emotions and time-honoured codes of appropriate conduct. Intuitions do not come to us from a Platonic or Kelsenian objective realm; they are forced into the deepest layers of our mind through parental, social, and historical conditioning.

Rorty depicts a "*societas* as opposed to a *universitas*... a society conceived as a band of eccentrics collaborating for purposes of mutual protection rather than as a band of fellow spirits united by a common goal... [where] morality is a matter of... 'we-intentions' [and] the core meaning of 'immoral action' is 'the sort of thing *we* don't do'."[354] The ground for any ethical theory and, more broadly, for any moral conviction, is the community or ethnos of which one is a member. Rorty himself, consistently with this view, states that he belongs to a specific ethnos, namely the Western, liberal one. More specifically, he is a member of the Western, and precisely North-American, liberal democratic community.[355]

Antirepresentationalism

Representationalism claims that human knowledge 'mirrors', 'reflects' or 'portrays' reality. The better and the more sophisticated our knowledge is, the more accurate our portrait of reality becomes. Natural science is the paradigmatic activity that depicts "facts" in an "objective" way, revealing them "as they are" in nature: "Some philosophers have remained faithful to the Enlightenment and have continued to identify themselves with the cause of science. They see the old struggle between science and religion, reason and unreason, as still going on, having now taken the form of a struggle between reason and all those forces within culture which think of truth as made rather than found."[356] They are wrong, however.

Rorty claims that "the very idea of such a representation [i]s pointless".[357] In his opinion, representationalism is just a bunch of metaphors inherited from Plato and Descartes, and a self-undercutting one. At a deeper layer of analysis, this epistemological tradition contains the seeds of scepticism *in se* [within itself]. As Rorty argues, if knowledge is a mirror, then the sceptic will always be able to ask: can we believe in what we see reflected? Isn't it distorted in some unpredictable way? How do we know it is not? And what lies between the mirror and the mirrored? How can we be certain that what we call "true" is actually true?

Rorty wants to wipe out this well-established approach to knowledge as intrinsically contradictory and hopelessly problematic. In his own words: "Truth cannot be out there – cannot exist independently of the human mind – because sentences cannot so exist, or be out there... The world does not speak. Only we do."[358] Those who do not accept this premise are going to be entangled in a web of irresolvable dichotomies. The mind-body problem, the realism-idealism opposition, the internalism-externalism conflict are all outcomes of this misleading approach. Rorty's alternative is a complete rejection of this hugely influential model, in favour of an alternative one derived from the classical US Pragmatists—mainly William James and John Dewey (1859–1952)—and from Charles Darwin (1809–1882).

According to these key sources of his, knowledge is not regarded as a mirror of reality, but as a *tool* (or set of tools) to cope with it. What matters for Rorty is that this tool can work successfully, i.e. that it satisfies our aims. If it works in a way (e.g. by way of a specific vocabulary) better than another because it is 'true', 'approximate', 'adequate', 'objective' or 'non-perspectival' is not a relevant point for Rorty. No definitive solution to this kind of concern can be found—scepticism being always possible—henceforth we should just stop wasting time about it, looking for the theory that shall clarify it once and for all. Praxis and literature, rather than theory and philosophical speculation about unfathomable epistemic conundrums, should become the predominant interest, if not the exclusive one. Theory is useful up to a certain extent, but the hope that it can lead us to some ultimate source of truth is a vain dream. According to Rorty, the belief in such a decisive possibility is but a vacuous, reassuring claim of the strongest rhetorical model adopted by our *ethnos*, which, as said, stems out of a long-lived "spectatorial" intellectual tradition, including Plato's, Aquinas' and Descartes' visual metaphors.[359]

Applying Thomas Kuhn's (1922–1996) *Structure of the Scientific Revolutions* to whole cultural shifts, Rorty argues that, as soon as the equilibrium of persuasive forces in the public domain should change, the weakness of the dominating model would grow and become eventually untenable, thus leading another rhetoric to take over as mainstream. Rorty is peremptorily candid about this point: theory, however articulate, is fundamentally nothing but a piece of rhetoric, whose logico-argumentative power cannot be sharply distinguished from persuasion. Under this respect, Rorty wants:

> *[U]s to see science and poetry, genius and psychosis – and, most importantly, morality and prudence – not as products of distinct faculties but as alternative modes of adaptation.... [since] there is no central faculty, no central self, called "reason".*[360]
>
> [...]
>
> *To say that we should drop the idea of truth as out there waiting to be discovered is not to say that we have discovered that, out there, there is no truth. It is to say that our purposes would be served best by ceasing to see truth as a deep matter, as a topic of philosophical interest, or "true" as a term which repays "analysis".*[361]

All that knowledge can do for sure is to help us deal with the environment in which we live, whereas any representational goal of its gets lost in the mists of sterile speculation.[362]

Liberalism

Rorty is a liberal or, at least, Rorty asserts repeatedly that he is a liberal.[363] *Contingency, Irony, and Solidarity* is meant to be his "liberal utopia", which is based upon:

> [T]he recognition... of a general turn against theory and toward narrative. Such a turn would be emblematic of our having given up the attempt to hold all the sides of our life in a single vision, to describe them with a single vocabulary... More important, it would regard the realization of utopias, and the envisaging of still further utopias, as an endless process – an endless, proliferating realization of Freedom, rather than a convergence toward an already existing Truth.[364]

Rorty is aware of the eccentricity of his project, which he nonetheless considers a worthy attempt to promote liberal values in the public sphere. In point of fact, he admits that "liberal ironists" like himself, as opposed to "liberal metaphysicians" like John Rawls or Jürgen Habermas (b. 1929),

> do not believe that there is... an order beyond time and change which both determines the point of human existence and establishes a hierarchy of responsibilities... are far outnumbered (even in lucky, rich, literate democracies) by people who believe that there must be one.[365]
> [...]
> Whereas the liberal metaphysician thinks that the good liberal knows certain crucial propositions to be true, the liberal ironist thinks the good liberal has a certain kind of know-how. Whereas he thinks of the high culture of liberalism as centering around theory, she thinks of it as centering around literature (in the older and narrower sense of that term – plays, poems, and, especially, novels).[366]

These considerable divergences notwithstanding, Rorty intends to defend "liberal institutions" rather "than the available alternatives", and to advocate "the sense of human solidarity which the development of democratic institutions has facilitated".[367] Deep and articulate reasons are not, after all, what moves most human beings into action or changing worldviews, attitudes and beliefs; more often than not, it is the emotional resonance accompanying some straightforwardly graspable reasons that obtains that result. In the grand scheme of rhetorical developments and changes determining the shape and vicissitudes of a culture, relevance trumps rigour every time, novels trump treatises, lofty ideals trump intricate reasonings, and changes of heart trump steadfast logical analyses. Consistently with this realisation, Rorty's moral and social commitment does not apply exclusively or even primarily to the high level of academic writing, but also and above all to the more ordinary level of active political life. "Redescription", namely the liberal ironist's mission of making non-ironic people become sceptical about themselves and therefore accept liberal principles more easily (e.g. tolerance, privacy, pluralism, personal freedom), is at least as much a practical tenet of his as a theoretical one.[368]

Ethnocentrism and Cruelty

If we look at the history and institutions of Rorty's liberal ethnos, then we can easily realise that cruelty is far from being the main concern of such a *Gemeinschaft*. The liberal, democratic ethnos, to which Rorty refers and in which Rorty lives, does not exclude cruelty nearly so thoroughly as Rorty says that it does.[369] For instance, capital punishment, brutal market competition, the humiliation of enduring poverty and unemployment, massive military operations, widespread police brutality, male rapes in prisons, boxing events, sadomasochistic sex-games, battery animal farming, and even animal mistreatment (e.g. rodeos) are often part of the culture and daily life of the ethnos that Rorty mentions, if not of its legal practices themselves.[370] In all these cases, a relevant component of cruelty is implied, whether it is regarded as *secondary* or as *intrinsic* to the enjoyment of the main goal (e.g. order, profit, protection of the State, retribution, aesthetic or erotic pleasure). In certain countries belonging to Rorty's Western ethnos, or whatever may be hypothesised this ethnos to be like, some of the aforementioned activities are banned by law as cruel, while in others they are not. Still, both in Europe and in America, cruelty seems not to be seen as the most serious concern inside the community.

Of course, I am not denying that it can be a relevant concern, but just as other important matters can be.[371] In the first place, the constitutions of such countries rarely refer to cruelty as one of their core-problems, the solution of which should be perceived as the distinctive task of the State.[372] In the second place, only certain forms of cruelty are persecuted by the State's institutions in order to be repressed (e.g. homicide, rape, battery, etc.) and even in these cases the State intervenes if and only if they infringe the constitutional rights of private citizens. In the third place, even if there are forms of cruelty which are reproved and punished, it is true that also other, non-liberal communities do the same. Aversion to cruelty is not a distinctive character of Western liberal democracies, at least more than it is among the Australian aboriginal tribes, Chinese Confucians or Tibetan Buddhists. Then, why does Rorty follow Judith Shklar and structures his definition of liberalism in close connection with the notion of cruelty, as patently exemplified by his claim [B]?[373]

Antirepresentationalism and Cruelty

Rorty's antirepresentationalism leaves us with a very weak notion of knowledge, because the notion of universal truth is declared fraudulent and obsolete. According to Rorty, we should have already left it far behind us. We have *us* and just *us*, our constructions, our traditions, our perspectives, our pieces of rhetoric—our truth. We should forget about the ancient philosophical and representationalist lexicon, inside which Rorty could be identified perhaps as a linguistic idealist of sorts, and accept his own new lexicon, which would transform us into "postmodern bourgeois... or evolutionary neo-pragmatists", or "liberal ironists":

> *I shall define an "ironist" as someone who fulfills three conditions: (1) She has radical and continuing doubts about the final vocabulary she currently uses, because she has been impressed by other vocabularies, vocabularies taken as final by people or books she encountered; (2) she realizes that arguments phrased in her present vocabulary can neither underwrite nor dissolve these doubts; (3) insofar as she philosophizes about her situation, she does not think that her vocabulary is closer to reality than others, that it is in touch with a power not herself.*[374]

As the stress in this passage on the ironist's "doubts" shows, there is unavoidably a veil of sceptical pessimism about our cognitive resources. The epistemological shift demanded by Rorty is not an easy step to take. Another indicator of such a fact lies in the use of the word "contingency", which initiates the very title of his most representative book. With it, Rorty emphasises the relevance of chance in describing our condition and its inescapable tragedy: cognitively, morally and existentially. Significantly, Rorty claims to adhere ideally to the Italian philosophical current called "weak thought" (*pensiero debole*), for which human rationality is incapable of any grand metaphysical grasp, as also taught by nihilists such as Friedrich Nietzsche and Martin Heidegger.[375] As Rorty writes: "The redescribing ironist, by threatening one's final vocabulary, and thus one's ability to make sense of oneself in one's own terms rather than hers, suggests that one's self and one's world are futile, obsolete, powerless."[376]

Yet, in spite of all this "doubting" and "powerlessness", Rorty builds an articulated ethical proposal. In *Contingency, Irony, and Solidarity*, Rorty claims that we all should be kinder to each other, as persuasively suggested by the most talented "poets" of our liberal community. These are people like Lev Tolstoy (1828–1910), Milan Kundera (b. 1929), William Faulkner (1897–1962), Vladimir

Nabokov (in his autobiography) and George Orwell, whose distinctive trait is "the fear of being, or having been, cruel"; they "dreaded... not having *noticed* the suffering of someone with whom one had been in contact".[377] Rorty states that he has exactly the same dream as Nabokov's father had: "the creation of a world in which tenderness and kindness are the human norm".[378] It is a dream that Rorty defends even if saying as well: "I do not think there are any plain moral facts out there in the world, nor any truths independent of language, nor any neutral ground on which to stand and argue that either torture or kindness are preferable to the other."[379] Rorty derives both an ethical and a political programme from the dream of Nabokov's father, namely a defence of liberalism as the best political arrangement to reduce cruelty, hence as the form of social life that better fulfils our best poets' advice. Furthermore, consistently with this programme, Rorty devoted himself to political action, mainly in the his native country, supporting specific political parties and policies (e.g. the institution of universal healthcare in the USA), following his parents' and grandparents' example.[380]

Critical Remarks on Ethnocentrism

A series of questions cannot but arise, at this point: why does Rorty get himself to step in such a direction? Ethical, political and existential commitments of this order of magnitude seem to require adequate metaphysical resources, so to speak, i.e. something conceptually stronger than mere irony, doubts and powerlessness.[381] If irony, doubts and powerlessness are the distinctive features of his liberalism, what on Earth may ever allow Rorty's rhetoric to be accepted by his human fellows, if at all listened to? And even if his fellows granted him some attention, what would the source of his rhetorical persuasiveness be like? Is it just a matter of having the right kind of poets, as the anti-theory, pro-literature claim [A] seems to imply, or does it hide something more? Even when following Rorty's "turn against theory and toward narrative",[382] we could wonder why our poets came up with such a *pro*-kindness literature in the first place. They despised cruelty: yes; but why? Poets are not expected to give us arguments and philosophical foundations; philosophers are, instead, at least as a courtesy to poets, who often rely upon them, e.g. Dante Alighieri on Thomas Aquinas, Ugo Foscolo (1778–1827) on Condorcet, George Bernard Shaw (1856–1950) on Friedrich Nietzsche, Luigi Pirandello (1867–1936) on Henri Bergson (1859–1941).

In the second place, one could still wonder why Rorty takes these poets as the 'right' kind of poets. It is an unresolved mystery why Rorty should not consider Sade, Giacomo Leopardi, Fyodor M. Dostoyevsky (1821–1881) or Louis-Ferdinand Céline (1894–1961) as equally distinctive poets of our ethnos. He surely mentions Charles Baudelaire (1821–1867), Friedrich Nietzsche and Vladimir Nabokov (in his literary works) as 'bad' poets, interested primarily in private perfection rather than public well-being, but why are they not *our* poets to the same extent as Gustave Flaubert (1821–1880) or Charles Dickens (1812–1870) are said to be?[383]

In addition to that, can Rorty support any positive plan in a credible way? Can he seriously have any sensible *pars construens* [constructive part], after professing his dismal plea for powerless ironism? After stating and accepting the severe theoretical limits of an antirepresentational, ethnocentric liberalism, what can give him any hope to succeed in its defence? As Michele Marsonet (b. 1950) argues, a Nazi philosopher could easily show that Rorty "cannot even argue in favour of [his own] convictions."[384]

In the first place, I believe Rorty's "ethnocentrism" to be misguided.

One thing is to talk about Germany, Wales, or Caithness; another is to talk about a "liberal ethnos" and "the West." What and where is this ethnos to which Rorty pays such high tributes? Where is this liberal, democratic "West"? Is it a myth or a real entity? And if it is real, which powers, legal institutions, political voices are meant to represent it? Rorty's writings are far from clear on this point. "Ethnos" and "ethnocentrism" are so generously used by Rorty in his writings, that both of them can be understood as dealing with a set of existing nations, an ideal form of political life, a literary canon, Western Europe and North America, North America alone, and much else.[385] Indeed, I confronted Rorty himself with the question "what do you mean with the term 'ethnos'?" He replied by confirming the very same vagueness that I am criticising: "Nothing too precise, or better, when I think about this term I do not mean much else than what you read in my books. *Ethnos* does not mean a precise model of social organization. It is meant to remind you that, once theoretical foundations have vanished, all that you have is your *Gemeinschaft*. It is the place where you were brought up, the place that you can call your own, at least in a broad sense."[386]

In the second place, I believe Rorty's "ethnocentrism" to be misguiding.

Firstly, due to the mentioned fuzziness of its referent, hardly any existing social community can be addressed through this concept. The rhetorical power of Rorty's ethnocentrism is unlikely to be of much use to any real advocate of solidarity, especially if compared to old-fashioned metaphysical ideas such as those of "the human being", "*le citoyen*" or "thy neighbour", which still pervade public debates.

Secondly, should Rorty's approach succeed, then ethical and political issues would become more and more issues about the exact definition of local identities. Who are "we"? Who is a member of our community? Who is to be allowed inside our tribe? Who are "they"? How can we turn "them" into some of "us"? Ethnocentrism, in this sense, could easily turn into a replica of nationalism, or of tribalism, or into a form of imperialism.[387] Cultural identities are only partially a matter of agreement or peaceful conversation. Quite often, in order to determine and nurture a sense of ethnicity, persuasive 'poetry' is accompanied by brute force, whether legal or illegal, and this applies to liberal democracy as well as to any other recognisable community. Perhaps, poetry itself is just an expression of force, insofar as a dominant section of the population selects the literary canon, the school programmes, and access to the media. Also, we should not forget that cultures are fluid, living entities, incorporating other potential or actual ethnoi and cultures, thus involving profound tensions. As Rorty himself recognises: "Socializing is often a matter of who manages to kill whom first."[388] After all, self-proclaimed "liberal democracies" have been more than ready to use bomb-raids and economic sanctions to countries trespassing on human rights: is this not "redescription"?

Thirdly, let us be so generous as to grant Rorty some agreement on the exact meaning of his "Western liberal ethnos", to which he says to belong.[389] We might identify it with the wealthy countries in Europe and North America, plus Australia and New Zealand, more or less another few. If we do so, then a clear defence of liberal democracy turns into a riddling historical morass. In the variegate existence of these nations, so many different forms of political life have succeeded one another, that gathering all of them under the same 'umbrella-ethnos' seems quite ludicrous. "Liberal" and "democracy" have hardly meant the same thing for the many members of such an ethnos, and probably still do. For instance: (1) some of these members would call themselves "liberal" and "democratic", even if they did not grant full civil rights to women as far as 1999;[390] (2) some others would use the adjective "social-democratic" and not "liberal" to describe their main constitutional roots;[391] (3) others still could say that they live under governments that regularly promote "bourgeois freedoms" through systematic oppression, whether by economic, judiciary or political means;[392] (4) whereas other "liberal democracies" have constitutions founded on God's will;[393] moreover (5), such a group of countries cannot be said to be the cradle of "liberal democracy" alone, insofar as fascism, white supremacy, State religion, socialism and populism may equally claim to be an essential part of their historico-political DNA.[394]

Critical Remarks on Antirepresentationalism

With regard to Rorty's "antirepresentationalism" and, as well, Rorty's "liberal irony", I believe such terms to be as misguiding as "ethnocentrism" is, insofar as they invoke a total 'poeticisation' of the ethical and political spheres (and the scientific one, too).[395] Instead of making the spectrum of plausible alternatives more nuanced, Rorty's rejection of the distinction between argumentation and persuasion 'jumps' into a modern version of emotivism.[396] Yet, this is not the only option available.

Masters of rhetoric such as Giambattista Vico[397] and, in more recent times, Chaïm Perelman,[398] should remind us that the choice is not between rigid Leibnizean *calculemus* [let's calculate] and behaviourist or Pavlovian TV ads whereby anything goes if adequately internalised by means of psychological association. These two dimensions do exist, but as the extreme poles of a series of degrees of probability (or verisimilitude) in which demonstration and persuasion co-operate. Aristotle himself, after all, had already distinguished between apodictic knowledge, which moves from certain premises (e.g. logic, geometry), and dialectical knowledge, which moves instead from uncertain and non-evident premises (e.g. jurisprudence, politics), and he discussed the degrees of verisimilitude and probability in between.[399] Rorty is too swift, too radical and too uncritical in his move from Cartesian clear and distinct ideas to sheer guts and hearts; or, if we like, from Plato's metaphysical absolutism to Protagoras' (487–412 BC) anthropological relativism. Rorty's "anti-rationalism" makes all realms of knowledge become the same sort of "conversation", a term he borrows from British conservative thinker Michael Oakeshott (1901–1990); it is a night in which all cows are black.[400] But this has not to be necessarily the case. Even in a non-dogmatic, or "antimetaphysical" context, one thing is an ordinary chit-chat, in which our prejudices are deployed without much care; whilst another is a "dialogue", in which our prejudices are brought onto the surface and scrutinised. We can converse in many ways.[401]

A further reason to see Rorty's "liberal irony" to be misguiding is that the total poeticisation of the ethical and political sphere does not leave us with any answer to the totalitarian threat. We can only appeal to the interlocutor's heart or, if we allow for a more generous interpretation of Rorty's message, to contingent pragmatic reasons. Still, in either or even in both instances, the totalitarian counterpart may refute our appeals, these being equally or less acceptable to her than her own stronger, seemingly reasoned grounds. Besides, she can demonstrate that there are pragmatic reasons to ground her own case too.[402] Yet, Vico and Perelman would remind us once more that we do not share with the interlocutor the emotional and the pragmatic spheres alone: we share also the sphere of rational debate, or we would not be able to communicate at all, nor would we recognise each other as counterparts; not even as fighting ones. Thus, instead of purging out possible means of interaction, we should use them together with those that we already have. Our faculties are not mutually exclusive. As Vico wrote: "All new arts and sciences should be added to those we already possess enlarging our stock of knowledge, as far as necessary, so that human wisdom may be brought to complete perfection."[403]

At a more fundamental level, "irony" and "liberalism" work against each other. Firstly, irony is disruptive of any strong conviction, whether liberal or not.[404] Secondly, if liberalism aims at reducing cruelty, then Rorty's irony is not liberal, for its declared task is to redescribe other people's vocabularies, thus causing them to experience pain, insofar as "most people do not want to be redescribed."[405] Thirdly, Rorty's attempted corrections to these two problems are inadequate. Rorty thinks, in fact, that a sharp split between the private and public spheres may be a good remedy. One can be a heartless cynical ironist in the private sphere, trying to accomplish only what her deeper desires are like, showing no moral concern of any sort. As for her private matters, the ironist may pursue her plans as a pure "self-creator", whatever they are like.[406] At the same time, though, when engaged in the public sphere, it is the shared set of values of her community that guides the ironist's conduct, i.e. the ironist loyally complies with the *mores maiorum* [ancestral habits; *mos* in the singular].[407] How plausible is this split, though? On the one hand, it is quite difficult to draw so sharp a line between private and public spheres, insofar as this is a legal distinction that varies with the social perception of what should be left out of the State's reach. Moreover, the redefinition and modification of such a line is one of the ironist's public tasks. Then, try to imagine the infernal divided self of the ironist. Endless doubts and confusion are likely to arise along the edge of such a thin, volatile, dividing line—when to behave according to one's own private projects? When to follow the tribe's public whims?[408] Disillusion, paralysis, hypocrisy, duplicity, calculated cynicism might all become her life companions.

Liberalism and Cruelty

Let us now go back to the core-issue of my investigation, namely the claims [A] and [B], which Rorty reformulates when stating that the "liberal ironist [wants] to separate the question 'Do you believe and desire what we believe and desire?' from the question 'Are you suffering?'."[409] Again, instead of suspending his judgement in the name of irony, doubt, and powerlessness, Rorty shows a deep ethical and political concern. As already seen, Rorty takes *aversion to cruelty* as the defining character of liberalism itself, whereas a conservative liberal, for instance, would have probably spoken of "coercion" and "negative freedoms"; or a progressive liberal would have mentioned "the common good" and "positive freedoms". The critical analysis presented in the previous paragraphs suggests that cruelty is Rorty's own distinctive main concern, rather than an exquisite, essential liberal concern. Rather than a characteristic feature of Western liberal democracies, cruelty is more typically Rorty's interpretative key for these societies (as well as Judith Shklar's and Nabokov's father's, as far as we can ascertain).

According to Rorty, we are moral if we reduce cruelty on the individual level, and we have a better community if we do the same on a collective scale. His political and epistemological positions share the same intimate inspiration: "antiauthoritarianism."[410] In effect, as the reformulation of [A] and [B] suggests, Rorty's account of cruelty orbits around two main concepts: "humiliation" and "being in pain", which he takes as *self-explanatory* and *evidently negative*. Thus, if we try to analyse a few more relevant passages in which Rorty somehow meditates upon such notions, we are able to detect their *common denominator*. Its discovery can then allow us to define that which makes all of them so bad, namely why they should be rejected, and why the anti-cruelty rhetoric supported by Rorty should be granted compelling force. In other terms, going through

Rorty's *Contingency, Irony, and Solidarity*, and particularly the section on "Private Irony and Liberal Hope", we can find passages that suggest that even the liberal ironist implicitly believes in a "final vocabulary", despite Rorty's explicit belief "that if doubt is cast on the worth of [its central] words, their user has no noncircular argumentative recourse... For in the ironist view... there is no such thing as a 'natural' order of justification for beliefs or desires."[411]

Incessantly, Rorty maintains that liberalism should be defended and promoted, since it preserves "the only important political distinction" namely "that between the use of force and the use of persuasion".[412] Liberalism does it in explicit favour of persuasion; and not only: liberalism is also the socio-political synonym for "peace", "wealth", and "the standard 'bourgeois freedoms'."[413] Thus, in few crucial lines, Rorty lists his own *desiderata* [desired items], which are the liberal ironist's *desiderata*, and which represent the source of strength of his own rhetoric *pro* kindness and *contra* cruelty. In fact, "persuasion rather than force", "peace rather than war", "wealth rather than poverty", "freedom rather than slavery", are the words that liberalism uses against its cruel adversaries: fascism, communism, theocracy, and absolutism.[414] For Rorty, the rhetorical power of these expressions is undeniable, at least inside the public sphere of his own ethnos. This explains why the "ironists who are also liberal think that such freedoms require no consensus on any topic more basic than their own desirability": liberal *desiderata* are strikingly desirable.[415] However, this paramount desirability has some specific origins that can explain and justify a wider appeal.

Rorty says that the liberal ironist does not need to obtain consensus on anything else but their desirability. He claims that the liberal ironist does not believe that their desirability possesses such an origin, a deeper ground for rational justification. The liberal ironist could be wrong, however, at least on the latter account. Whether aware of it or not, Rorty himself opens his philosophy to a foundational option when he writes: "What binds societies together are common vocabularies and common hopes. The vocabularies are, typically, parasitic on the hopes."[416] Rorty's distinction between a moral-political lexicon and a set of social hopes seems to imply some sort of terrain upon which ironic liberalism itself stands; something prior to the formulation of a liberal rhetorical nexus of moral values and political goals. To a deeper scrutiny, the supposedly circular liberal vocabulary appears to rest upon some pre-liberal hopes or, if preferred, upon some pre-liberal *desiderata*. Unintentionally, Rorty denounces the presence of a compelling element which sustains *any* vocabulary and decides its fortune, insofar as the good life of a host is a necessary condition for the parasite's own one. In other words, Rorty's thought does entail some sort of "natural order of justification for beliefs or desires" insofar as: [I] he refers to the mentioned deeper set of pre-liberal hopes; and insofar as [II] he says that *parasitic* liberalism defends them better than any other political model, and [III] *ergo* that we *ought to* defend liberalism as the best lexicon available. There is a *ground* beneath the liberal rhetoric that Rorty purports and it is, as far as I can determine, also *universal*:

> *[The liberal ironist] thinks that what unites her with the rest of the species is… susceptibility to pain and in particular to that special sort of pain which the brutes do not share with the humans – humiliation… [i.e.] a common selfish hope, the hope that one's world – the little things around which one has woven into one's final vocabulary – will not be destroyed.*[417]

Rather patently, we are allowed to infer the universality of the ground which lies beneath the liberal lexicon, since Rorty envisages a common bond among all human beings ("our species"): "humiliation" and, more generally, our ability to experience *pain*. Here is the conceptual mass around which Rorty's politics and ethics revolve. *Nobody wants to suffer*: this is Rorty's grounding universal *datum*. Humans do not like pain at all. Quite constantly, if they can, they avoid it. Hence, *avoidance of pain* becomes the *conditio sine qua non* [condition without which] for any *desideratum* to gain substantial social consensus: "Solidarity has to be constructed… in the form of an ur-language which all of us recognise when we hear it."[418]   And what is better heard than pain? Bentham and the utilitarians, who have been part and parcel of the liberal camp since the early 19th century, have always claimed as much.

It must be noted that Rorty states that "pain is nonlinguistic."[419] But this is simply false. Pain is linguistic insofar as it can be expressed *via* consistent reactions to it, which can be understood conceptually by the suffering person herself and by other humans, as far as they have been successfully socialised. Some reactions to pain may be nonlinguistic (e.g. crying or arc-reflex spasms), some may be quasi-linguistic (e.g. the mourning chant of Jordanian women, or shouting aloud), but some are exquisitely linguistic (e.g. cursing at God, telling one's doctor what is wrong, undergoing therapeutic analysis, Boethius' self-soothing writing of *De consolatione philosophiae*). Taking only the first kind of cases as the only cases existing is a double mistake. First of all, such a move contradicts a huge amount of empirical evidence; and it equally contradicts our commonsensical understanding of our human fellows. Secondly, it shows very little respect to those who are trying to let us know that they are in pain and that we should do something about it. If we are liberals, as Rorty claims to be, and we do want to oppose cruelty, then we should take their problem seriously.

In Rorty's philosophy, perhaps tacitly, liberals operate a sort of logical deduction from what all humans seem to fear: pain. If we all are afraid of pain, then no better society can be built than the one which minimises it. Consistently, liberalism wants to liberate 'us'— and possibly 'them' as well—from the threat of cruelty, humiliation: *pain*. With "them" I mean the members of other ethnoi, or even animals, since pain: "is what we human beings have that ties us to the nonlanguage-using beasts [and to] victims of cruelty, people who are suffering."[420] There can are cases in which pain is inescapable, or even called upon oneself in the name of self-perfection. Throughout history, there have been individuals who have undergone painful redescriptions of their system of belief in view of a newer and higher one. However, these Promethean or eccentric figures, people like Friedrich Nietzsche or Ignatius of Loyola (1491–1556), are *exceptions*, perhaps exceptional and, more significantly, they do not contradict the truth that *pain is bad* and that we regularly try to *avoid* it. In fact, they have followed their drive to self-perfection *in spite of* the pain that it involved and in spite of the *demand* that such pain had on them: *don't do that!* Besides, the fact that Rorty stands against Nietzsche and Loyola as potential threats to peaceful, *painless* co-existence in society, choosing instead the call for solidarity coming from Dewey and Orwell, shows how the pain-avoidance principle has not only a grounding character, but also a normative one. It is normative because it fosters the creation of norms, either social or individuals, aimed at guiding behaviour. Certainly, it does guide Rorty's.

Two Contradictions

I borrow the following understanding of normativity from the Danish-American philosopher Christine Korsgaard (b. 1952), who writes in her book, *The Sources of Normativity*:

> *A living thing is an entity whose nature it is to preserve and maintain its physical identity. It is a law to itself. When something it is doing is a threat to that identity and perception reveals that fact, the animal finds it must reject what it is doing and do something else instead. In that case, it is pain. Obligation is the reflective rejection of a threat to your identity. Pain is the unreflective rejection of a threat to your identity. So pain is the perception of a reason.*[421]

Pain gives the sufferer a reason, upon which the subject must act as legislator, in order for her to deliberate whether to endure such state of affairs or to escape from it. In this manner, pain turns into the source of normativity, for it is the fosterer of the subject's self-regulation. If this account of normativity is correct, then Rorty's ethical and political reflections, which, as seen, orbit around the notion of pain, do hide a normative character inside themselves. Moreover, due to the universality and to the grounding character of pain, both of which have been outlined in my previous paragraphs, it is possible to state that Rorty's "liberal utopia" rests upon a universal normative ground. If we understand metaphysics as the domain of meta-empirical, comprehensive accounts, i.e. the grand narratives *à la* Plato, Hegel, or Spengler that Rorty *qua* neo-pragmatist wants to dismiss, then he himself is appealing to an account of this sort. Independently of one's own ethnos and its contingent vocabulary, this universal ground of "susceptibility to pain" tells every sentient creature to avoid pain, whenever possible. In the specific case of human beings, pain determines what ought to be done, as well as it directs what kind of society should be built by them. Pain does not appeal to Rorty's enlightened intellectual. Pain *cries* at the individual or at the collectivity: "stop it! don't do that!" The ironist herself, in spite of all, listens to this voice. The ironist being a liberal one, moreover, will certainly oppose cruelty. In other words, the claim [B] involves the use of a justifying "final" lexicon, which is based upon pain, and which contradicts the anti-metaphysical nature of the claim [A]. To conclude, then, we are in the presence of a *formal* contradiction.

Yet, the reader might disagree with Korsgaard's account of the ultimate source of normativity, as well as with the understanding of "normativity" and "metaphysics" used here. In either case, the critique moved to Rorty in the previous paragraph would fall: no formal contradiction can be detected. Or, at least, it would be not the same as the one that I have outlined. A *performative* contradiction could be detected instead. Rorty's liberalism wants to create a society freed from "the brutes" and implement our "selfish hope that one's world will not be destroyed",[422] as highlighted in [II]. Destruction or, in Rorty's terms, "redescription", is a painful, humiliating, cruel action, which calls for limitation, restraint, moderation, tolerance and civility. In truth, it must be used with extreme care, possibly only in order to avoid worse forms of destruction. This is why the liberal ironist should use it only to promote liberalism and its values, which give us the chance "to make new and different things possible and important",[423] such as "'domination-free communication'... as the aegis under which society is to become more cosmopolitan and democratic".[424] The ironist herself is warned not to abuse of the "awareness of the power of redescription", since "most people do not want to be redescribed"; quite the opposite:

> *[They] want to be taken on their own terms – taken seriously just as they are as they talk. The ironist tells them that the language they speak is up for grabs by her and her kind. There is something potentially very cruel about this claim. For the best way to cause people long-lasting pain is to humiliate them by making the things that seemed most important to them look futile, obsolete, and powerless.*[425]

Why should the ironist bother, though? Why should the ironist be a *liberal* ironist? Rorty himself considers the hypothetical case of non-liberal ironists:

> *One can easily imagine an ironist badly wanting more freedom, more open space, for the Baudelaires and the Nabokovs, while not giving a thought to the sort of thing Orwell wanted: for example, getting more fresh air down into the coal mines, or getting the Party off the backs of the proles. This sense that the connection between ironism and liberalism is very loose... is what makes people distrust ironism in philosophy and aestheticism in literature as "elitist".*[426]

In spite of this imaginary scenario, Rorty does not retire into an ivory tower and into exquisite elitism. On the contrary, he becomes a spokesman for Orwell's concerns.

Concluding Remarks

Orwell used an essentialist lexicon, and specifically a democratic socialist lexicon. In his words and thoughts, he was as foundationalist, representationalist and metaphysical as his political battles required and as the socialism of his day invariably was.

Rorty, on his part, tells the reader more or less the same things as Orwell did, but with the words of a contingent, ethnocentric, antirepresentationalist and poeticised lexicon. Why? Unless the ironist's beliefs imply that pain has a *normative* force, why should she care? How would she know that cruelty must be avoided? The only answer that I can find is that a pain-centred foundational assumption is lurking behind Rorty's concern about cruelty and his commitment in favour of liberalism as aversion to cruelty. In Rorty's writings, whether he is aware of it or not, pain is the source of normativity directing his public activity. And even if this original element is buried under heaps of appeals to sentiment and rhetorical aptitude, any philosophically trained ear cannot but detect its reverberation.

Chapter 9: Enemies of Interculturalism. The Economic Crisis in Light of Xenophobia, Liberal Cruelties and Human Rights

In this final chapter I briefly discuss the notion of *interculturalism*, or at least some aspects relating to it within "the Nordic context", such as:

- Failure in the "inclusion" of "minorities" (cf. below "Xenophobia"); and
- Some of the defining "political... cultural, and economical [*sic*]" features of liberalism, which is today's political norm in Nordic states too, i.e.:
  - Its contrariness to cruelty (cf. "Cruelty"); and
  - Its inherent inability to get rid of it (cf. "Liberalism").[427]

From a connotative point of view, interculturalism is the combination of different cultures into one. From a denotative point of view, I am myself a living token of interculturalism in a Nordic country. I am a citizen of two nations, i.e. Italy and Iceland; I was born and raised as a Catholic in Italy; educated in Italy, Iceland and Canada; I am married to a Presbyterian Scot and the father of two trilingual bi-confessional children; I have been a philosophy teacher in Canada, France, Great Britain, Italy and, above all, Iceland, the country where I have lived since 2003; and I am an active scholar taking part in symposia and workshops abroad—thus far, in three different continents (i.e. Europe, America, Asia). Under all these guises, I have witnessed the beauty, but also the ugliness, of intercultural dialogue and lack thereof. Cruelty, in effect, can find room also in this context.

Xenophobia

At the onset of the international economic crisis in 2008, I witnessed as well how quickly a minority or an individual 'stranger' can be bullied, marginalised or excluded from a social body, to which she may believe to belong by virtue of, *inter alia*: learning the local language, befriending local inhabitants, participating in the local community life, contributing to the local economy, paying into the nation's social insurance fund, fulfilling the legal conditions for asylum under human rights and humanitarian law, or raising children in the host community. No social setting is too low or too high for these unpleasant phenomena to happen. Albeit being a member of the lofty academic domain nominally devoted to universality—think of the meaning of the Latin word *universitas*—, I too was harassed by an Icelandic colleague, who spared no opportunity to make me and other foreign-born staff members feel unwelcome, including a former US citizen that had resided in Iceland for more than thirty years. Eventually, this colleague of mine was formally reprimanded by the rector of my university, though never fired; as a result, as far as I have been able to gather, he keeps finding victims to bully, though not exclusively along ethnic lines. But I do not wish to dwell on a personal incident, which serves only as a vivid example of the ugliness mentioned above. Rather, I would like to tackle a little-known aspect of the so-called "second Icelandic miracle".

After the first miracle, which consisted in the boom phase of a boom-bust cycle caused by standard neoliberal policies of liberalisation and privatisation over the 1990s and 2000s, a second miracle was performed. The new—now old—left-wing government of the country brought Iceland back to prosperity in just four years (2009–2013), i.e. about the time that the newly privatised three largest banks of the country had taken to bring it to a globally televised meltdown (2003–2008). Apart from many Icelanders, who have proven quite oblivious to the considerable achievements of that left-wing cabinet, international observers were amazed. In particular, some of the policies implemented—which included letting over-indebted private banks fail, freezing sovereign debt obligations, and the reintroduction of capital controls were so unorthodox that they led Nobel-laureate US economist Paul Krugman (b. 1953) to praise Iceland as a "dramatic demonstration of the wrongness of conventional wisdom in these times [of crisis]".[428] Yet, amongst the policies implemented, there was also a sinister tightening of immigration rules, which led to the impossibility for non-EU residents to have their residency permits issued or renewed. We do not know how many people did not enter Iceland or left it because of this reason, as the research in this matter is limited.[429] Nevertheless, the effects of this change of policy were timidly acknowledged in the 2011 national report for the Office of the High Commissioner for Human Rights at the United Nations.[430]

I am not interested in discussing the legal specifics of the case, though later on I touch upon the issue of human rights. Rather, I take the tightening of immigration rules as an example of a characteristic feature of economic crises. By spreading panic and insecurity about the future, these crises lead to a stronger albeit possibly instrumental claim to national identity and self-protection (e.g. "Iceland for the Icelanders", or "Finland for the Finns"); a sharper division between 'us' and 'them'; and the exclusion of human beings that are more easily excluded than others, i.e. the most vulnerable members of society. Fuelled by the fear that economic uncertainty inevitably generates, xenophobia rarely targets white-collar foreign bankers or well-paid financial experts and consultants, who may actually have a share of penal responsibility *vis-à-vis* the economic crisis. On the contrary, it targets regularly foreign men, women and children belonging to the working class, if not to the underclass of the illegally unemployed, unemployed and petty criminals, who often live in the peripheries of urban centres, the *banlieues* of Paris, or of Malmö. Whether physical, psychological or institutional, there is always a modicum of violence in xenophobia, which operates through a plethora of means, e.g. verbal abuse, social isolation, contrary legislation, reduced employment opportunities, ill-treatment by police and court officers, assault by street thugs. Often, this violence targets individuals that are perceived as foreign and yet have done no harm to anyone else, that is, *innocent* persons.

Cruelty

Social psychologists Kemp, Brodsky and Caputo report violence to innocents to be one of the most commonly recognised forms of *cruelty*. Although they conclude that no clear-cut definition can be provided by mapping and comparing usages of "cruelty" and "cruel", which vary enormously both historically and geographically, causing pain to innocents is fairly uncontroversial.[431] Philosophers and political theorists often limit themselves to mapping and comparing linguistic usages too, just like social scientists. I, for one, have done it *qua* intellectual historian, as chapter 4 exemplifies. Yet, philosophers and other theorists often attempt something more daring, i.e. to provide *essential definitions*, which aim at capturing the fundamental traits of a given phenomenon, or those traits that, if absent, make a certain thing into another. This is something that philosophers and political theorists still do, sometimes in indirect ways, since they try not to make use of metaphysically burdensome 'essentialisms'. For one, late Harvard professor Judith Shklar defined cruelty in at least two ways, as we read in chapter 3. On their basis, joined later by Richard Rorty, she championed the so-called "liberalism of fear", i.e. an advocacy of Western-style liberalism as the best bulwark against cruelty which, following Montaigne, Shklar claimed to feed on *fear*. All these three thinkers regarded fear as the most illiberal feeling in the human psyche, since "fear destroys freedom", i.e. the central value of the liberal tradition.

Liberalism

I certainly agree with the three of them on fear's ability to destroy freedom—and much else. Yet, is their understanding of liberalism warranted? It is my reasoned belief that it is not. Liberalism is not capable of opposing cruelty effectively; nor fear, for that matter. Let me explain briefly why. First of all, we saw in chapter 3 that John Kekes argues how, by granting the individual more personal freedom, liberalism grants *de facto* each and every one of us more scope to do what we like, hence also more scope for cruelty. I need

162

not remind the reader of the unspeakable tragedies of Oslo and Utøya, back in 2011, which were the result of one man choosing *freely* the path of cruelty, that is, free from, say, the constant scrutiny from public authorities that the average East German citizen would have had to endure before 1990. Secondly, liberal institutions include penal ones, which are constitutionally mandated to mete out punishments.

Now, as necessary and even as beneficial as the lawfully sanctioned punishments may be, they are a form of cruelty. We read in chapters 3 and 4 that not even the great penal reformer of the Age of Enlightenment, Cesare Beccaria, thought it possible for punishments to be purified entirely from cruelty. More rational methods could be implemented, unnecessary pain could be avoided; yet, the *nature* of penal sanctions remained, in his view, quintessentially cruel.

Significantly, the great Norwegian criminologist Nils Christie, whom we encountered in chapter 6, argued that standard penal justice is *doubly* cruel because it does not take into genuine consideration: (1) the alternatives available (e.g. treatment, conciliatory debate or reconciliation, public apology and restitution, forgiveness); and (2) it ignores decades of studies showing that penal justice as we know it, has never attained its prime official end, i.e. social order. Thirdly, as briefly hinted in chapter 3, Beccaria acknowledges the cruelty inherent to the economic system that liberals—himself included—have been defending since the 17th century, i.e. as *per* the political writings of John Locke (1632–1704). In *On Crimes and Punishments* (1764), the chapter about the crime of "theft" reads in its entirety:

> *[T]his is generally the crime of misery and despair, the crime of that unhappy part of men to whom (the terrible, and perhaps unnecessary right to) property has allowed nothing but a bare existence, {and since fines only increase the number of criminals above the original number of crimes, and take bread from the innocent in order to take it from the villains} the most fitting punishment shall be the only sort of*

slavery that can be called just, namely the temporary enslavement of the labour and person of the criminal to society, so that he may redress his unjust despotism against the social contract by a period of complete personal subjection.[432]

Beccaria is here admitting that the liberal conception of the economy, insofar as it institutes private property rights, is responsible for the conditions of misery that make this crime emerge. The right to own property privately, "terrible" and "perhaps unnecessary" as it is, lies at the core of the liberal political, legal and economic system. Yet, it is also the source of pauperism, for it allows certain members of society to have much more than they need, while leaving others' needs unmet. In turn, pauperism is the source of theft. And theft, which is indeed a crime, has to be repressed *via* "atrocious punishments". It may sound surprising that Beccaria could speak so loudly of the horrors of private property, but it is often forgotten that 18th-century liberals had often a drier and more candid perception of things than most of their contemporary heirs, who still retain the original faith in both penal justice and private property, but tend to couch it in anodyne terms. Besides, the horrors of private property were not a new discovery: Jesus of Nazareth (4 BC–30 AD), Blaise Pascal and John Milton (1608–1674) had already warned humankind about the disruptive and sinful temptations of material wealth—Mammon being a demon from Hell.

Concluding Remarks (on Human Rights)

With all its flaws, we may still deem the liberal system better than the alternatives. I am not going to enter this dispute here. Quite simply, I want to let the reader reflect on some of the strings that are attached to the political, legal and economic system championed by Rorty and glorified by Fukuyama after the collapse of the Soviet bloc. Indeed, the on-going economic crisis, with its socially destructive effects, is one of such strings. What I am re-stating here, in sum, is the wisdom of a well-known adagio: *there is no such thing*

164

as a free lunch. Do not think that I am being dismal or pessimistic. It may well be true that there is no such thing as a free lunch. Life involves hard times and painful choices. Still, through collective action and/or inaction, the menu of the lunch for which we pay can be changed. Think, for one, of the imposition of austerity measures in great part of Europe as a result of the economic crisis of 2008. Somehow, it has been argued, the emergency situation, or conditions of *force majeure* [superior force], require Europe's societies to re-trench from human rights provisions, despite these being sanctioned in binding international treaties, especially but not exclusively the *European Convention on Human Rights* (signed 1950, effective 1953) and the UN's *International Covenant on Economic Social and Cultural Rights* (s. 1966, e. 1976). This retrenchment is pursued in order to honour the repayment requests of the member States' institutional investors and recovery the collapsing private banking sector. Yet, as the Icelandic example demonstrates, the same emergency situation can be appealed to in order to make the property rights of State creditors, wealthy investors and private banks secondary, while prioritising precisely those economic, social and cultural rights to which much of Europe has legally committed itself. Even in times of crisis, to a reasonable extent, we can be masters of our fate. If anything, we can choose at least how to suffer.

Endnotes

Comprehensive of bibliographic information, electronic sources included.

[1] The sole tome devoted to it is Michael Trice, *Encountering Cruelty: The Fracture of the Human Heart*, Leiden: Brill, 2011.

[2] Richard Rorty, *Contingency, Irony, and Solidarity*, Cambridge: Cambridge University Press, 1989, 73.

[3] Richard Rorty, *Achieving Our Country. Leftist Thought in Twentieth-Century America*, Cambridge: Harvard University Press, 1998, 89 & 81.

[4] Cf. the archive of all speeches delivered by Donald Trump during his presidential campaign (<https://www.donaldjtrump.com/media/category/speeches>) and a 2016 selection of his statements by *The Telegraph* (<http://www.telegraph.co.uk/news/2016/03/22/donald-trumps-most-outrageous-quotes/>).

[5] I write "front stage" because Trump's predecessor did not halt, say, police violence in the US or the bombing of the populations of foreign countries by US drones (e.g. Libya, Syria, Iraq, Afghanistan, Pakistan, Yemen), but he never spoke of such issues in a cavalier manner. Concerning the US military foreign sites, cf. Department of Defense, *Base Structure Report – Fiscal Year 2015 Baseline*. <http://www.kritisches-netzwerk.de/sites/default/files/us_department_of_defense_-_base_structure_report_fiscal_year_2015_baseline_-_as_of_30_sept_2014_-_a_summary_of_the_real_property_inventory_-_206_pages.pdf>.

[6] Regarding the final bibliography and the endnotes accompanying this book, I made use of the Chicago Style Citation standard, i.e. the most common one among Anglophone academic philosophers, though purged of some of its more quixotic aspects. I do believe that, thanks to the information provided, the reader should find it very easy to retrieve any or all of the sources utilised for this book.

[7] Blaise Pascal, *Pensieri. Testo francese a fronte*, Milan: Rusconi, 1993 [Copy B, 1669].

[8] Definitions, quasi-definitions, and pseudo-definitions of cruelty are rare but not absent in the philosophical literature of the 20th century. We find some in the writings of André Dinar (*Les auteurs cruels*, Paris: Mercure de France, 1972[1942]), Antonin Artaud (*The Theater and its Double*, translated by Mary Caroline Richards, New York: Grove Press, 1958[1938]), Philip Hallie (*The Paradox of Cruelty*, Middletown: Wesleyan University Press, 1969), Gilles Deleuze and Félix Guattari (*Anti-Oedipus*, translated by Robert Hurley, Mark Seem and Helen R. Lane, New York: The Viking Press, 1977[1972]), Judith Shklar (*Ordinary Vices*, Cambridge: Belknap, 1984), Clement Rosset (*Joyful Cruelty: Toward a Philosophy of the Real*, translated by David F. Bell, New York: Oxford University Press, 1993[1988]), Tom Regan (*The Case for Animal Rights*, Berkeley: University of California Press, 1983), Richard Rorty (*Contingency, Irony, and Solidarity*, Cambridge: Cambridge University Press, 1989) and John Kekes ("Cruelty and Liberalism", *Ethics*, 106(4), July 1996, 834–44).

[9] As cited in Alicia A. Caputo, Stanley Brody and Simon Kemp, "Understanding and Experiences of Cruelty: An Exploratory Report", *The Journal of Social Psychology*, 140(5), 2000, 649–60, 1st section.

[10] Ibid.

[11] Ibid.

[12] Ibid.

[13] Thomas Aquinas, *Summa Theologica*, translated by Fathers of the English Dominican Province, 1920[ca. 1268], part II of part II, question 159, art. 1, <http://www.newadvent.org/summa/>. In this book I utilise the standard scholarly referencing system for Aquinas' *Summa*.

[14] Ibid., art. 1 & 2.

[15] Niccolò Machiavelli, *The Prince*, translated by W.K. Marriott, 1908[1515], chapter VIII, <http://www.constitution.org/mac/prince00.htm>.

[16] Michel de Montaigne, *The Complete Es*says, translated by Donald Frame, Stanford: Stanford University Press, 1998[1580], II, 27 & 11. Given the great variety of editions of Montaigne's essays, I do not refer to page numbers and use the standard scholarly system instead, i.e. book and essay number.

[17] Ibid., II, 11.

[18] Thomas Hobbes, *Leviathan*, London: Andrew Crooke, 1651, part I, chapter XV, <http://socserv2.socsci.mcmaster.ca/econ/ugcm/3ll3/hobbes/Leviathan.pdf>.

[19] As cited in *British Moralists 1650-1800*, edited by D.D. Raphael, Indianapolis: Hackett, 1991, vol. 1, 334–5.

[20] Ibid., vol. 2, 72.

[21] Montesquieu, *The Spirit of Laws*, translated by Thomas Nugent, New York: Cosimo, 2011[1748], book VI, chapter 1, §12.

[22] Adam Smith, *Theory of Moral Sentiments*, 6th edition, London: A. Millar, 1790, part II, section 2, chapter 3, §21, <http://www.econlib.org/library/Smith/smMS.html>.

[23] Adam Smith, *An Inquiry into the Nature and Causes of the Wealth of Nations*, edited by Edwin Cannan, Indianapolis: The Online Library of Liberty, 1901[1776], book I, chapter 11, §263, <http://www.econlib.org/library/Smith/smWN.html>.

[24] Donatien Alphonse François, Marquis de Sade, *La Philosophie dans le boudoir ou Les Instituteurs immoraux*, Paris: Larousse, 1966[1795], 139–40 (translation mine).

[25] Giacomo Leopardi, "Dialogo di Plotino e di Porfirio", in *Operette Morali*, 1836, <http://www.leopardi.it/operette_morali.php> (translation mine).

[26] Ibid., "Detti memorabili di Filippo Ottonieri" (translation mine).

[27] Ibid., "Dialogo di Tristano e di un amico" (translation mine).

[28] Friedrich Nietzsche, *Ecce Homo & The Antichrist*, translated by Thomas Wayne, New York: Algora, 2004[1888 & 1895], "Genealogy of Morals – A Polemic", 81.

[29] Friedrich Nietzsche, *Beyond Good and Evil*, translated by Judith Norman, Cambridge: Cambridge University Press, 2002[1886], §229.

[30] Friedrich Nietzsche, *Daybreak*, translated by R.J. Hollingdale, Cambridge: Cambridge University Press, 1997[1881], §18.

[31] Cf. Giorgio Baruchello, *Understanding Cruelty: From Dante to Rorty*, Ph.D. Thesis, University of Guelph, 2002, for a comprehensive, detailed and nuanced account.

[32] Cf. Philip P. Hallie, *The Paradox of Cruelty*, Middletown: Wesleyan University Press, 1969.

[33] Cf. Ted Honderich, "After the Terror: A Book and Further Thoughts", *The Journal of Ethics*, 7, 161–81.

[34] Cf. Philip P. Hallie, *The Paradox of Cruelty*.

[35] I believe the best philosophical explanation of the issues of denotation and meaning to be Michael Polanyi's, as succinctly introduced and summarised in Walter B. Gulick, "Polanyi's Theory of Meaning: Exposition, Elaboration, and Reconstruction", *Polanyiana* 2(4) & 3(1), 1992–3, 32–40.

[36] Cf. Gilles Deleuze and Félix Guattari, *Anti-Oedipus*.

[37] Cf. Plato, *Plato in Twelve Volumes*, translated by Paul Shorey, W.R.M. Lamb, R.G. Bury *et al.*, London: William Heinemann, 1925–69[4th century B.C.]: cf. *Protagoras* 345b, *Theaetetus* 199e, *Laws* 9.863c & 5.731c. Given the great variety of editions of Plato's dialogues, I use the standard scholarly referencing system for his works, i.e. the so-called "Stephanus" system (from Renaissance French scholar Henri Estienne, who published in Geneva in 1578 the collected works of Plato in both the original Greek and the Latin translation).

[38] Cf. Aristotle, *Complete Works*, revised Oxford translation edited by Jonathan Barnes, Princeton: Princeton University Press, 1984[4th century BC]: cf. *Problems*, Book XVI, 928b23 to 929a5; *Metaphysics*, Book V, 1022b4 to 14; *Nichomachean Ethics*, Book VII, 1148b18-34; *Eudemian Ethics*, Book II, 1220b18, 1222b5–14. As already done for Plato, so do I utilise here too the standard scholarly referencing system for Aristotle, i.e. the so-called "Bekker numbers" (from August Immanuel Bekker, philologist and critic at the Prussian Academy of Sciences, who published between 1831 and 1836 the standard edition of the complete works of Aristotle).

[39] Cf. especially Emmanuel Levinas, "The Ego and the Totality", in *Collected Philosophical Papers*, translated by Alfonso Lingis, Dordrecht: Kluwer, 1993[1954], 25–46.

[40] Ibid.

[41] Ibid.

[42] Emmanuel Levinas, *Totality and Infinity*, translated by Alfonso Lingis, Pittsburgh: Duquesne University Press, 1969[1961], 134.

[43] Scott Miller and Sarah A. Ogilvie, Refuge Denied: The St. Louis Passengers and the Holocaust. Madison: University of Wisconsin Press, 2006.

[44] Cf. Roy Baumeister, *Evil: Inside Human Violence and Cruelty*, New York: Freeman, 1997.

[45] Emmanuel Levinas, *Totality and Infinity*, 131–2.

[46] Emmanuel Levinas, *Collected Philosophical Papers*, translated by Alfonso Lingis, Dordrecht: Kluwer Academic Press, 1993[1987], 25–46.

[47] Ibid.

[48] Emmanuel Levinas, *Totality and Infinity*, 134.

[49] Friedrich Nietzsche, *Daybreak*, §30.

[50] Ibid.

[51] Ibid.

[52] Ibid.

[53] Ibid.

[54] Ibid.

[55] Ibid.

[56] Ibid.

[57] Ibid.

[58] Ibid.

[59] Ibid.

[60] Ibid.

[61] Ibid.

[62] Ibid.

[63] Ibid.

[64] Ibid.

[65] Ibid.

[66] Ibid.

[67] Ibid.

[68] Ibid.

[69] Ibid.

[70] William Paley, *A View of the Evidences of Christianity*, London: Society for Promoting Christian Knowledge, n.d.a., 340.

[71] Ibid.

[72] Ibid.

[73] William Edward Hartpole Lecky, *The History of the Rise of Rationalism*, 2 vols., New York: D. Appleton, 1884, vol. 1, 356.

[74] Cf. William Edward Hartpole Lecky, *History of European Morals from Augustus to Charlemagne*, 2 vols., New York: D. Appleton, 1875.

[75] Ibid., vol. 1.

[76] Ibid., 139.

[77] Ibid.

[78] Ibid.

[79] Ibid.

[80] Ibid.

[81] Ibid.

[82] Ibid.

[83] Ibid.

[84] Ibid.

[85] Ibid.

[86] Ibid.

[87] Ibid.

[88] Ibid., 140.

[89] Friedrich Nietzsche, *Twilight of the Idols Idols: or How to Philosophize with a Hammer*, translated by Duncan Large, Oxford: Oxford University Press, 2009[1889], "Maxims and Arrows", §8.

[90] Niccolò Machiavelli, *The Prince*, chapter XVII.

[91] Friedrich Nietzsche, *Beyond Good and Evil*, §9.

[92] Ibid.

[93] Thucydides, *History of the Peloponnesian War*, chapter 17, as cited in *Sources for the History of Western Civilization*, edited by Michael Burger, Toronto: University of Toronto Press, 2015[431 BC], 2nd ed., vol. 1, 146.

[94] James Madison, *Federalist Papers*, #10, 22 Nov. 1787, <http://www.constitution.org/fed/federa10.htm>.

[95] Cf. Friedrich Nietzsche, *The Will to Power*, translated by Walter Kaufmann and M.J. Hollingdale, New York: Random House, 1968[1901].

[96] Thomas Hobbes, *Leviathan*, part I, chapter X.

[97] Ibid., chapter XI.

[98] William Shakespeare, *Complete Works*, Champaign IL: Project Gutenberg, 1994, <http://davidlucking.com/documents/Shakespeare-Complete%20Works.pdf>.

[99] Giacomo Leopardi, *Operette morali,* "Dialogo delta Natura e di un islandese" (translation mine).

[100] Ibid. (translation mine).

[101] Friedrich Nietzsche, *Ecce Homo & The Antichrist*, "Genealogy of Morals – A Polemic", 81.

[102] Friedrich Nietzsche, *The Complete Works of Friedrich Nietzsche*, 13 vols., "The Greek State. Preface to an Unwritten Book", translated by Oscar Levy, New York: MacMillan, 1911[1871], vol. 2, 8.

[103] Gilles Deleuze and Félix Guattari, *Anti-Oedipus*, 144–5.

[104] Gilles Deleuze and Félix Guattari, *A Thousand Plateaus: Capitalism and Schizophrenia*, translated by Brian Massumi, Minneapolis: University of Minnesota Press, 1987[1980], 425.

[105] Emmanuel Levinas, *Totality and Infinity*, 142.

[106] Cf. Martin Heidegger, *Being and Time*, translated by John Macquarrie and Edward Robinson, San Francisco: Harper, 1962[1927], 57, 187, 189 & 356.

[107] Hans Jonas, *The Phenomenon of Life: Toward a Philosophical Biology*, New York: Harper and Row, 1963, 215.

[108] Ibid., 233.

[109] Ibid.

[110] Ibid.

[111] Cf. Lyall Watson, *Dark Nature: A Natural History of Evil*, New York: Harper Perennial, 1996.

[112] Lucius A. Seneca, *Epistles*, 10 vols., translated by R.M. Gummere, Cambridge, MA: Harvard University Press, 1917–25[ca. 20–65 AD], vol. 2, 515.

[113] Luciano Floridi and J.W. Sanders, "Artificial Evil and the Foundation of Computer Ethics", *Ethics and Information Technology*, 3(1), 2001, 55.

[114] Cf. Kenneth F. Schaffner and H. Tristram Engelhardt, *Philosophy of Medicine*, London: Routledge, 1998.

[115] Rachel Cooper, "Disease", *Studies in History and Philosophy of Biological and Biomedical Sciences*, 33, 2002, 263. Birth and, if applicable, death dates are not provided here for 'minor' contemporary scholars and scientists (whom might be deemed 'major' by future generations).

[116] Bjørn Hofmann, "On the Triad Disease, Illness and Sickness", *Journal of Medicine and Philosophy*, 27(6), 2002, 651.

[117] Ibid., 657.

[118] Michael Baum, "Pro-Genetic Testing Should Be Discouraged", *European Journal of Cancer*, 34, 2005, 87.

[119] Leslie J. Blackhall, Gelya Frank, Sheila Murphy and Vicki Michel, "Bioethics in a Different Tongue: The case of truth-telling", *Journal of Urban Health: Bulletin of the New York Academy of Medicine*, 78(1), 2001, 59.

[120] Cf. Susan Sontag, *Illness as Metaphor*, New York: Farrar, Straus & Giroux, 1978, chapter 8.

[121] Cf. Michel Foucault. *Folie et déraison: Histoire de la folie à l'âge classique*, Paris: Gallimard, 1972 (2nd ed.).

[122] Richard Rorty, *Contingency, Irony, and Solidarity*, xvi.

[123] Cf. Cesare Beccaria, *On Crimes and Punishments and Other Writings*, translated by Richard Davies, Cambridge: Cambridge University Press, 1995[1764].

[124] Judith Shklar, *Ordinary Vices*, 9.

[125] Judith Shklar, "The Liberalism of Fear", in *Liberalism and the Moral Life*, edited by N. Rosenbaum, Harvard: Harvard University Press, 1989, 29.

[126] Judith Shklar, *Ordinary Vices*, 2.

[127] Ibid., 5.

[128] Cf. John Kekes, "Cruelty and Liberalism", *Ethics*, 106, 1996, 834–44.

[129] Ibid., 835.

[130] Ibid.

[131] Ibid.

[132] Cesare Beccaria, *Dei delitti e delle pene e Commento di Voltaire*, Rome: Newton, 1994[1764], 22 & 30 (translation mine).

[133] Ibid., 42 (translation mine).

[134] Ibid. (translation mine).

[135] This motto is attributed by historians to Cork-born jurist John Philpot Curran (1750–1817).

[136] Páll S. Árdal, *Passions, Promises and Punishments*, Reykjavík: University of Iceland Press, 1998, 62.

[137] Cf. David Hume, *A Treatise of Human Nature*, Harmondsworth: Pelican, 1969[1738–40], 586–635.

[138] As cited in Kate Kellaway, "At home with his worries", *The Guardian*, 16 September 2001.

[139] Richard Rorty, *Contingency, Irony, and Solidarity*, xv–i.

[140] Judith Shklar, *Ordinary Vices*, 237.

[141] Richard Rorty, *Contingency, Irony, and Solidarity*, xiv.

[142] Ibid.

[143] Ibid., 160.

[144] Ibid., xv–i.

[145] As cited in ibid., 31.

[146] Baruch Spinoza, *Ethics,* in *Collected Works*, translated by Edwin Curley, Princeton: Princeton University Press, 1988[1677], §3.38.

[147] Cf. Alicia A. Caputo, Stanley Brody and Simon Kemp, "Understanding and Experiences of Cruelty: An Exploratory Report"; and Simon Kemp, Stanley Brody and Alicia A. Caputo, "How Cruel is a Cat Playing with a Mouse? A Study of People's Assessment of Cruelty", *New Zealand Journal of Psychology,* 26(2), 1997, 19–24.

[148] *Job*, 30.21. I assume the reader to be familiar with Biblical abbreviations.

[149] Lucius A. Seneca, *De Clementia*, translated by John W. Basore, London: Heinemann, 1928–35[55 AD], II.iv.1–4. Whenever possible, given the great variety of editions over the centuries of Latin classics, I use the standard referencing system for such sources.

[150] Ibid.

[151] Ibid.

[152] Ibid. I.xxiv.1–xxv.2.

[153] Ibid. I.xii.1–4.

[154] Ibid. I.ii.2–iii.3.

[155] Aquinas, *Summa Theologica*, part II of part II, question 159, art. 1.

[156] Ibid.

[157] Ibid., art. 2.

[158] Ibid.

[159] Thomas Hobbes, *Leviathan*, part I, chapter VI.

[160] As cited in *British Moralists 1650–1800*, vol. 1, 334–5.

[161] As cited in ibid., vol. 2, 72.

[162] Thomas Hobbes, *Leviathan*, part I, chapter XV.

[163] Michel de Montaigne, *The Complete Essays*, II, 27.

[164] Ibid., II, 11.

[165] Ibid.

[166] Montesquieu, *The Spirit of the Laws*, book VI, chapter, 12; book XV, chapters 1, 7 & 15; book XXVI, chapter 22.

[167] Cf. Voltaire, *Oeuvres complètes de Voltaire*, edited by Louis Moland, Paris: Garnier, 1877[1769].

[168] Adam Smith, *The Theory of Moral Sentiments*, part V, chapter I, §25.

[169] Ibid., part VI, chapter III, §12.

[170] Adam Smith, *An Inquiry into the Nature and Causes of the Wealth of Nations*, book IV, chapter 8, §17.

[171] Ibid., book V, chapter 2, §§116 & 125.

[172] Ibid., book I, chapter 11, §263.

[173] Ibid., book II, chapter I, §27.

[174] Pietro Verri, *Osservazioni sulla tortura* Rome: Newton, 18 (translation mine).

[175] Cesare Beccaria, *Crimes and Punishments*, translated by James Anson Farrer, London: Chatto & Windus: 1880[1764], 140–1.

[176] Ibid., 243.

[177] Marquis de Condorcet, *Esquisse d'un tableau historique des progrès de l'esprit humain*, Xème & IIème époque, 2004[1793–4], <http://www.eliohs.unifi.it/testi/700/condorcet/index.html> (translation mine).

[178] Immanuel Kant, *Zum ewigen Frieden. Ein philosophischer Entwurf*, part II, chapter 2, §3 (translation mine).

[179] Immanuel Kant, *Philosophy of Law. An Exposition of the Fundamental Principles of Jurisprudence as Science of Right*, translated by W. Hastie, Edinburgh: T. & T. Clark, 1887[1796], part II, section I, chapter 49, art. E.

[180] C.f. note 124.

[181] C.f. note 125

[182] Judith Shklar, *Ordinary Vices*, 237.

[183] Giacomo Leopardi, *Operette morali*, "Dialogo di Tristano e di un amico" (translation mine).

[184] Tom Regan, *The Case for Animal* Rights, Berkeley: University of California Press, 1983, 197–8 (emphases in the original).

[185] Francis Fukuyama, *The End of History and the Last Man*, New York: The Free Press, 1992.

[186] Judith Shklar, *Ordinary Vices*, 3, 7 & 44.

[187] Philip P. Hallie, *The Paradox of Cruelty*, 14.

[188] *Encyclopaedia of Ethics* (edited by Lawrence C. Becker, New York: Garland, 1992), s.v. "Cruelty", by Philip P. Hallie, 229–31, 229.

[189] Philip P. Hallie, *Lest Innocent Blood Be Shed: The Story of the Village of Le Chambon, and How Goodness Happened There*, New York: Harper & Row, 1985[1979], 2.

[190] Philip P. Hallie, *The Paradox of Cruelty*, 5–6.

[191] Ibid., 13–4 & 29–31.

[192] Ibid., 22–4.

[193] Ibid., 15–20.

[194] Ibid.

[195] Ibid., 20–2.

[196] André Dinar, *Les auteurs cruels*, 7.

[197] Philip P. Hallie, *The Paradox of Cruelty*, 70–5.

[198] Ibid., 41 & 46.

[199] Ibid., 43.

[200] Ibid., 42 & 50.

[201] Ibid., 48.

[202] Ibid., 55–8 & 60–2.

[203] Ibid., 33.

[204] Ibid., 79–82.

[205] Niccolò Machiavelli, *The Prince*, chapter XVII.

[206] Jacques Derrida, *Without Alibi*, translated by Peggy Kamuf, Stanford: Stanford University Press, 2002[2000], 252.

[207] Gilles Deleuze and Félix Guattari, *Anti-Oedipus*, 144.

[208] Clément Rosset, *Joyful Cruelty*, 17.

[209] Ibid., 17–20.

[210] Ibid., 76.

[211] Ibid., 98 (emphases in the original).

[212] Antonin Artaud, *The Theater and its Double*, 101–3 & 85.

[213] Ibid., 102.

[214] Ibid., 114 (emphasis in the original).

[215] Sade, *La Philosophie dans le boudoir ou Les Instituteurs immoraux*, 139 (translation mine).

[216] Ibid., 140–1 (translation mine).

[217] Friedrich Nietzsche, *Daybreak*, §18.

[218] Friedrich Nietzsche, *Beyond Good and Evil*, §229.

[219] Friedrich Nietzsche, *Thus Spake Zarathustra*, translated by Thomas Common, 1891[1883–91], part IV, §65, section 1 (generally known and translated as *Thus Spoke Zarathustra*).

[220] Cf. Fouad Kalouche, *Ethics of Destruction: The Path towards Multiplicity. The Cynics, Sade, and Nietzsche*, PhD Thesis, SUNY Binghamton, DA3006909, 2001; and José Lasaga-Medina, "El mas alla libertino", *Revista Anthropos*, 192(3), 2001, 171–84.

[221] Sade, *Histoire de Juliette ou les Prospérités du vice*, 2007[1797–1801], part I, <http://www.sade-ecrivain.com/juliette/juliette.htm> (translation mine).

[222] Ibid. (translation mine); it is interesting to notice how Sade's account contains glaring germs of much 19th-century political and social thought, such as class warfare (Proudhon, Marx and Engels), social equilibrium (Comte, Durkheim and Pareto), and natural struggle (Darwin, Nietzsche and Spencer).

[223] Ibid. (translation mine).

[224] Sade, *La Philosophie dans le boudoir ou Les Instituteurs immoraux*, 138 (translation mine).

[225] Sade, *Histoire de Juliette ou les Prospérités du vice*, part I (translation mine).

[226] Sade, *La Philosophie dans le boudoir ou Les Instituteurs immoraux*, 140 (translation mine).

[227] Ibid., 136 (translation mine).

[228] Ibid., 137–8 (translation mine).

[229] Ibid., 139 (translation mine).

[230] Ibid., 142 (translation mine).

[231] Friedrich Nietzsche, *Human, All Too Human. A Book for free Spirits*, translated by R.J. Hollingdale, Cambridge: Cambridge University Press, 2005[1878–80], §99 (emphases in the original).

[232] Ibid.

[233] Ibid., §101.

[234] Ibid.

[235] Friedrich Nietzsche, *Daybreak*, §18.

[236] Friedrich Nietzsche, *The Will to Power*, translated by Anthony M. Ludovici, 1910[1888], §29, <https://archive.org/details/TheWillToPower-Nietzsche>.

[237] Ibid.

[238] Friedrich Nietzsche, "Schopenhauer as Educator", *Untimely Meditations*, translated by R.J. Hollingdale, Cambridge: Cambridge University Press, 1984[1874], part III, chapter IV.

[239] Friedrich Nietzsche, *Thus Spake Zarathustra*, part I, §3.

[240] Friedrich Nietzsche, *Beyond Good and Evil*, §55.

[241] Friedrich Nietzsche, *On the Genealogy of Morals*, translated by Carol Diethe, Cambridge: Cambridge University Press, 2006[1887], 1st essay, §11 (emphasis in the original).

[242] Friedrich Nietzsche, *Thus Spake Zarathustra*, part I, §13.

[243] Ibid.

[244] Friedrich Nietzsche, *Human, All Too Human*, §104.

[245] Ibid. (emphasis in the original).

[246] Sade, *La Philosophie dans le boudoir*, 142–3 (translation mine).

[247] Ibid., 136 (translation mine).

[248] As cited in Francine DuPlessy-Grey, *At Home with the Marquis De Sade,* New York: Simon & Schuster, 1998, 337.

[249] Ibid., 338–9.

[250] Ibid.

[251] Ibid.

[252] Friedrich Nietzsche, "The Greek State. Preface to an Unwritten Book", 7.

[253] Ibid.

[254] Ibid.

[255] Herbert Spencer, *The Man* versus *the State*, Caldwell: The Caxton Press, 1960[1884]), 110.

[256] Cf. Adolf Hitler, *Mein Kampf,* translated by James Murphy, 1939[1924], chapter 4 <http://www.greatwar.nl/books/meinkampf/meinkampf.pdf>.

[257] Cf. Ayn Rand, *Atlas Shrugged,* New York: Random House, 1957; and her 1944 letter to Leonard Read (*The Letters of Ayn Rand*, 172): "Personally, I am very much impressed with the quotations from William Graham Sumner", i.e. the leading social Darwinist in 19th-century US.

[258] Friedrich Nietzsche, *Human, All Too Human*, §72.

[259] Ibid., §81.

[260] Ibid.

[261] Dante Alighieri, *Inferno*, (canto) VI, (verses) 7–9 and 13–18: *I was in the third circle, where it rains/Eternally, icily and implacably; weight and direction are invariable./Cerberus, a cruel and outlandish beast,/Barks like a dog, from his three throats, at those/Who, under that downpour, are there submerged/Red eyes he has, and unctuous beard and black/And belly large, and armed with claws his hands/He rends the spirits, flays, and quarters them* (translation mine).

[262] Cf. Paget Toynbee, "Boccaccio's Commentary on the Divina Commedia", *The Modern Language Review*, 2(2), 1907, 97–120.

[263] The *Inferno* is subdivided into three main sections, on the basis of the gravity of the sins committed against reason, namely the attribute that makes humans similar to God. The first group is that of "incontinence", namely those who allowed passions to rule over reason. The second is that of "mad bestiality" or "violence", namely those who used reason as a tool in the hands of sheer passion. The third is that of "fraud" or "malice", namely those who used reason coldly to achieve evil ends.

[264] The *Inferno* develops as a descending conic structure under the city of Jerusalem. Satan, who lies at the bottom of it and who is stuck into a frozen lake forever, is exactly at the centre of the Earth. On the other side, i.e. the southern hemisphere, emerges the conic mountain of the *Purgatorio*, which surged out of the surface when the Earth moved away from Satan, while this was falling from heaven with the other rebellious angels, for even the Earth itself did not want to touch him.

[265] Respectively: self-murderers, *Inferno*, XIII; liars, *Inferno*, XXVI; and the three worst sinners of all times endlessly eaten by Satan himself: Brutus, Cassius (the murderers of Caesar, i.e. offenders of secular justice at the highest degree) and Jude (the man who betrayed Jesus, i.e. the worst offender of divine justice).

[266] Cf. Dante Alighieri, *Inferno*, VI, 94–115.

[267] Mt, 3.11.

[268] Cf. Carl L. Becker, *The Heavenly City of the 18th-Century Philosophers*, New Haven: Yale University Press, 1961, 33–46; and Norman Hampson, *The Enlightenment. An evaluation of its assumptions, attitudes and values*, London: Penguin, 1982, 16–31.

[269] As cited in *Philosophical Perspectives on Punishment*, edited by Gertrude Ezorsky, Albany: SUNY, 1972, 3 (emphasis added).

[270] Jeremy Bentham, *An Introduction to the Principles of Morals and Legislation*, 1997[1789], chapter 14, §16 (emphasis added), <http://www.earlymoderntexts.com/assets/pdfs/bentham1780.pdf>.

[271] Ibid., chapter 13, §2.

[272] John Kekes, "Cruelty and Liberalism", 841–2.

[273] Cesare Beccaria, *Dei delitti e delle pene e Commento di Voltaire*, chapter XII (translation mine).

[274] Ibid., "Introduction to the reader" (translation mine); Bentham will famously recover this motto by Beccaria.

[275] Ibid., chapter XXVIII (translation mine).

[276] Ibid. (translation mine).

[277] Ibid. (translation mine).

[278] As cited in *Philosophical Perspectives on Punishment*, 81.

[279] Repeating an older Christian claim (e.g. Ancius Manlius Severinus Boetius, *De consolatione* philosophiae, 523 AD, <http://www.portalefilosofia.com/biblioteca/materiale/cons_lat.pdf>) Erich Gabert argues that justice can only be done if the guilty person recognises her fault and, morally speaking, self-imposes the punishment (cf. *Punishment in Self-Education and in the Education of the Child*, Forest Row: Steiner Schools Fellowship Publications, 1972). Unaware of its Medieval roots, Gabert styles Dostoyevsky's Raskolnikov as the literary prototype of this understanding of justice, which he retrieves also in Blaise Pascal and Ludwig Wittgenstein.

[280] As cited in *Philosophical Perspectives on Punishment*, 4–5.

[281] As cited in *Law, Morality, and Rights*, edited by Michael Stewart, Dodrecht: Reidel, 1983[1979], 394–5.

[282] Ibid.

[283] Ibid.

[284] Ibid.

[285] On the received dominant views of retributivism and utilitarianism cf. widespread standard textbooks such as R.M. Baird and S.E. Rosenbaum, (eds.), *Philosophy of Punishment*, New York: Prometheus Books, 1988; and A.J. Simmons, M., Cohen, J. Cohen, and C.B. Beitz, (eds.), *Philosophy and Public Affairs*, Princeton: Princeton University Press, 1995.

[286] Concerning voices agreeing on the non-resolved and perhaps non-resoluble dichotomy between retribution and utility, cf. Heinrich Oppenheimer, *The Rationale of Punishment*, Montclair: Patterson Smith, 1975; Nigel Walker, *Punishment, Danger and Stigma. The morality of criminal justice*, Oxford: Basil Blackwell, 1980; and Wesley Cragg, *The Practice of Punishment*, London: Routledge, 1992.

[287] Nils Christie, *Limits to Pain*, Oslo: Universitetsforlaget, 1981, 10–1.

[288] Ibid.

[289] Given Christie's use of "man" and male pronouns, I am following suit in this chapter.

[290] For a history of 18th-century theories of punishment cf. James Heath, *Eighteenth Century Penal Theory*, Oxford: Oxford University Press, 1963.

[291] Nils Christie, *Limits to Pain*, 31.

[292] Ibid., 38–43.

[293] Ibid., 44 & 57.

[294] Ibid., 31–5.

[295] Ibid.

[296] Cf. Harry E. Barnes, *The Story of Punishment. A Record of Man's Inhumanity to Man*, Montclair: Patterson Smith, 1972; Calvert R. Dodge, *A World Without Prisons*, Lexington: Lexington Books, 1979; and *The Sociology of Punishment*, edited by Dario Melossi, Aldershot: Dartmouth, 1998.

[297] Nils Christie, *Limits to Pain*, 32.

[298] John K. Galbraith, *Money. Whence It Came, Where It Went*, Boston: Houghton-Mifflin, 1975, 230.

[299] Nils Christie, *Limits to Pain*, 14–9.

[300] Ibid.

[301] Ibid.

[302] Ibid., 36.

[303] Ibid., 46.

[304] Cf. Nils Christie, *Crime Control as Industry: Towards Gulags, Western Style*, New York: Routledge, 2000[1996], in which he reports on escalating such phenomena in privatised penal institutions, primarily in the US and the UK.

[305] Nils Christie, *Limits to Pain*, 47–52.

[306] Nils Christie, *Limits to Pain*, 74.

[307] Cf. Leslie T. Wilkins, *Punishment, Crime, and Market Forces*, Aldershot: Dartmouth, 1991, on market reforms as criminogenic. Christie's focus is not placed on white-collar crime, which, in the wake and aftermath of the 2008 financial crisis, has proven disruptive on a colossal scale.

[308] Nils Christie, *Limits to Pain*, 58.

[309] Ibid., 65.

[310] Ibid., 20–6.

[311] Ibid.

[312] Ibid. Ted Honderich, *Punishment*, London: Hutchinson, 1969, had already denounced these limitations.

[313] Nils Christie, *Limits to Pain*, 20–6.

[314] Ibid., 24–5. Knowledge of these phenomena is not new. Cf. Ira P. Robbins, "Managed Health Care in Prisons as Cruel and Unusual Punishment", *The Journal of Law and Criminology*, 90(1), 1999, 195–237, reporting on the regularly worsened standards of privatised healthcare in prisons; and H. Schwartz, "A Person is a Person and a SHOPS is Not", *Values and Ethics in Health Care*, 5, 1980, 226–8, reporting on the dreadful consequences of under-funding and under-staffing public services.

[315] Nils Christie, "Answers to Atrocities", 2002 [modified manuscript from paper presented at the 35th Biannual Congress of the Institute of Sociology, Krakow, July 11-16 2001; made available to me by the author]. In it, Christie argues that truth-commissions and conciliatory mediation would be the most effective instruments against terrorism: "we might in the end have no better solution than forgiveness."

[316] Nils Christie, *Limits to Pain*, 92–116.

[317] Ibid., 75–80.

[318] Ibid., 81.

[319] Ibid., 81–91

[320] Cf. Giles Playfair and Derrick Sington, *The Offenders. The Case Against Legal Vengeance*, New York: Simon & Schuster, 1957, in which it was already argued that crime is a "human case" and that, as such, abstract laws can never fit adequately.

[321] In "Answers to Atrocities", Christie argues that crime is an evil performed by a legal person. Legal persons are more than just these acts, however: their sphere of agency is capable of other and better actions than just the crime. After all, as no painter paints all the time, so no criminal commits crimes all the time. The institution of public justice should take into account this fact and try to nurture the alternative directions of the person's agency, rather than locking the person (and its own goals) inside the sole crime committed. To reduce the person and the function of the institution to appendixes of the crime means to give primacy to evil and renounce the good.

[322] Cf. John Braithwaite, *Restorative Justice and Responsive Regulation*, Oxford: Oxford University Press, 2002; Lawrence Sherman and Heather Strang, *Restorative Justice: The Evidence*, London: The Smith Institute, 2007, <http://www.restorativejustice.org/10fulltext/restorative-justice-the-evidence>; and *The Forgiveness Project* (2004–2014), <http://theforgivenessproject.com>.

[323] Nils Christie, *Limits to Pain*, 92–113.

[324] Ibid., 115.

[325] Ibid., 97–8.

[326] Ibid., 99–104.

[327] Ibid.

[328] Ibid.

[329] Ibid., 105–18.

[330] Ibid., 98.

[331] Ibid., 113–6.

[332] Ibid. This applies to vengeful individuals as well as to vengeful communities. As European literature has often portrayed in novels and plays, a small ethnos can turn into small hell for the outcast, even when a crime has not been really perpetrated. Personal traits that collide with the homogeneity of the community can turn into the worst stigma imaginable, whether they are homosexuality, adultery, or mere beauty.

[333] Ibid. On this point, Christie remarks that this paradox reinforces the notion, neglected by "classical" criminology, according to which emotional participation is intrinsic to justice.

[334] In "Answers to Atrocities", Christie states that, throughout is long career, he has never met a "monster".

[335] Nils Christie, *Limits to Pain*, 113–6.

[336] Cf. Marvin Henberg, *Retribution. Evil for Evil in Ethics, Law, and Literature*, Philadelphia: Temple University Press, 1990, which considers Dante's *Inferno* the *paradigmatic* example of retributive justice.

[337] Dante Alighieri, *Inferno*, XX, 7–15 & 19–25. *And people saw I through the circular valley/Silent and weeping, coming at the pace/Which in this world the Litanies assume/ As lower down my sight descended on them/Wondrously each one seemed to be distorted/From chin to the beginning of the chest/ For tow'rds the reins the countenance was turned/And backward it behoved them to advance/As to look forward had been taken from them.../As God may let thee, Reader, gather fruit/From this thy reading, think now for thyself/How I could ever keep my face unmoistened/When our own image near me I beheld/Distorted so, the weeping of the eyes/Along the fissure bathed the hinder parts* (translation mine).

[338] Ibid., 25–30. *Truly I wept, leaning upon a peak/Of the hard crag, so that my Escort said/To me: Art thou, too, of the other fools?/ Here pity lives when it is wholly dead;/ Who is a greater reprobate than he/Who feels compassion at the doom divine?* (translation mine).

[339] Ibid., XI, 93 (translation mine).

[340] Cf. ibid., II & *Purgatorio*, XVI.

[341] Cf. *Inferno*, III & *Paradiso*, VII.

[342] Cf. *Inferno*, XI, XIV and XIX.

[343] Ibid., XIV, 6.

[344] Richard Rorty, "Una filosofia tra conversazione e politica", interview by Giorgio Baruchello, *Iride*, 11(25), 1998, 457–8 (translation mine).

[345] Cf. Richard Rorty, *Objectivity, Relativism, and Truth. Philosophical Papers – Vol. I*, Cambridge: Cambridge University Press, 1991.

[346] Cf. Arthur Schopenhauer, *Über die Universitäts-Philosophie*, Berlin: Hoof, 2014[1851].

[347] Cf. Evandro Agazzi, "Analogicità del concetto di scienza. Il problema del rigore e dell'oggettività nelle scienze umane", in *Epistemologia e scienze umane*, edited by V. Possenti, Milan: Massimo, 1979, 57–76.

[348] Percy W. Bridgman, "On Scientific Method", *Reflections of a Physicist*, 1955, <https://www.lhup.edu/~dsimanek/bridgman.htm>.

[349] What I report here is the content of private exchanges between us.

[350] C.f. note 144.

[351] Richard Rorty, *Contingency, Irony, and Solidarity*, i.

[352] Cf. Richard Rorty, *Objectivity, Relativism, and Truth*, 31–4, 198–202 & 213–4; *Essays on Heidegger and Others. Philosophical Papers – Vol. II*, Cambridge: Cambridge University Press, 1991, 25–6, 197–8; and *Achieving Our Country*, 180ff.

[353] Richard Rorty, *Contingency, Irony, and Solidarity*, 58–9.

[354] Ibid., 59.

[355] Ibid., 93.

[356] Ibid., 3.

[357] Ibid., 4.

[358] Ibid., 5–6.

[359] It is by writing about this tradition that Rorty made his breakthrough in the academic philosophy at the end of the 1970s, cf. his book *Philosophy and the Mirror of Nature*, Princeton: Princeton University Press, 1979.

[360] Richard Rorty, *Contingency, Irony, and Solidarity*, 33.

[361] Ibid., 8.

[362] Cf. also Richard Rorty, *Objectivity, Relativism, and Truth*, 1–17, 21–34, 63–77, 151–61; *Essays on Heidegger and Others*, 9–26; *Truth and Progress. Philosophical Papers – Vol III*, Cambridge: Cambridge University Press, 153–63.

[363] Cf. also Richard Rorty in Herman J. Saatkamp, *Rorty and Pragmatism. The Philosopher Responds to His Critics*, Nashville: Vanderbilt University Press, 1995, 45–60.

[364] Richard Rorty, *Contingency, Irony, and Solidarity*, xvi.

[365] Ibid., xv (emphasis in the original).

[366] Ibid., 93.

[367] Ibid., 197.

[368] Cf. Richard Rorty, "Una filosofia tra conversazione e politica", 477–81 (translation mine).

[369] Richard Rorty, *Contingency, Irony, and Solidarity*, 198.

[370] For instance, at the time of publication of the original article, Italy had no capital punishment, plus it prohibited extradition to countries where capital punishment was enforced, as well as it had no interdiction regarding violent sexual games between consenting adults; the UK condemned all S&M as assault and contemplated capital punishment in the case of treason.

[371] Rorty's broad and imprecise connotation of "ethnos" justifies my shift from the conceptual level of the anthropologist's ethnos to that of the political student's State; cf. Richard Rorty, "Una filosofia tra conversazione e politica", 482 (translation mine).

[372] Cf. and compare the US constitution (8th amendment) and in the Italian one (2nd section).

[373] Similar considerations apply to Judith Shklar's "liberalism of fear".

[374] Richard Rorty, *Contingency, Irony, and Solidarity*, 73.

[375] Richard Rorty, *Essays on Heidegger and Others*, 10.

[376] Richard Rorty, *Contingency, Irony, and Solidarity*, 90.

[377] Ibid., 157 (emphasis in the original).

[378] Ibid., 160.

[379] Ibid., 173.

[380] Cf. Richard Rorty, "Trotsky and the Wild Orchids", 1992 (available also in *Philosophy and Social Hope*, London: Penguin Books, 1999), <http://www.philosophy.uncc.edu/mleldrid/cmt/rrtwo.html>.

[381] Cf. also Richard Rorty, *Achieving Our Country*, 1–38 & 111–24; and *Truth and Progress*, 307–26.

[382] Richard Rorty, *Contingency, Irony, and Solidarity*, xvi.

[383] On "liberal utopia", "irony" and "redescription" cf. also Richard Rorty, *Essays on Heidegger and Others*, 66–82, 164–76.

[384] Michele Marsonet, "Richard Rorty's Ironic Liberalism: A Critical Analysis", *Journal of Philosophical Research*, XXI, 1996, 391.

[385] On how vague "ethnos", "community", "we" etc. can be, cf. Richard Rorty, *Objectivity, Relativism, and Truth*, 76–7 & 103–4; and *Achieving Our Country*, 35–8.

[386] Richard Rorty, "Una filosofia tra conversazione e politica", 482 (translation mine).

[387] Cf. Susan Haack and John Kekes in Herman J. Saatkamp, *Rorty and Pragmatism*, 126–47 & 834–7.

[388] Richard Rorty, *Contingency, Irony, and Solidarity*, 185.

[389] Richard Rorty, *Objectivity, Relativism, and Truth*, 206–7.

[390] It is only as of 1999 that all Swiss cantons have been granting universal suffrage, irrespective of gender, despite the long democratic history of the Federal Republic of Helvetia.

[391] E.g. Finland and Norway.

[392] E.g. Russia and the USA.

[393] E.g. Canada and the USA.

[394] E.g. Italy, Spain, Greece and the USA.

[395] On the topic of ethics and politics, cf. Richard Rorty, *Contingency, Irony, and Solidarity*, 60–1, and *Truth and Progress*, 180–5; on the topic of science, cf. *Objectivity, Relativism, and Truth*, 31–34 & 157–58.

[396] On argumentation and persuasion, cf. Richard Rorty, *Contingency, Irony, and Solidarity*, xv, 16–20, 23–34 & 51–3.

[397] Cf. Giambattista Vico, *On the Most Ancient Wisdom of the Italians*, translated by L.M. Palmer, Ithaca: Cornell University Press, 1988[1710], chapter 1.

[398] Cf. Chaim Perelman and Lucie Olbrechts-Tyteca, *The New Rhetoric: A Treatise on Argumentation*, translated by John Wilkinson, Notre Dame: University of Notre Dame Press, 1969[1958], 53–6, 61–2 & 256.

[399] Cf. Edwin Wallace, *Outlines of the Philosophy of Aristotle*, Oxford: James Parker, 1976[1880].

[400] Richard Rorty, *Objectivity, Relativism, and Truth*, 60–2.

[401] Cf. Jeff Mitscherling, "Philosophical Hermeneutics and 'The Tradition'", *Man and World*, 22, 1989, 247–50.

[402] Cf. Michele Marsonet, "Richard Rorty's Ironic Liberalism".

[403] Giambattista Vico, *On the Study Methods of Our Time*, translated by Elio Gianturco, Ithaca: Cornell University Press, 1990, 3–4.

[404] Cf. David F. Dudrick, "Rorty on the 'Private-Public' Distinction", in *Proceedings and Addresses of the APA*, 74(4), 2001, 92–3.

[405] Richard Rorty, *Contingency, Irony, and Solidarity*, 89.

[406] Ibid., 85.

[407] Ibid., 196–9.

[408] Cf. David F. Dudrick, "Rorty on the 'Private-Public' Distinction".

[409] Richard Rorty, *Contingency, Irony, and Solidarity*, 198.

[410] Richard Rorty, "Una filosofia tra conversazione e politica", 457–8 (translation mine).

[411] Richard Rorty, *Contingency, Irony, and Solidarity*, 73 & 83.

[412] Ibid., 84.

[413] Ibid.

[414] Rorty uses often the term "totalitarianism" as to describe any *illiberal* political system that opposes "Welfare-State capitalism" (Richard Rorty in Herman J. Saatkamp, *Rorty and Pragmatism*i, 57).

[415] Richard Rorty, *Contingency, Irony, and Solidarity*, 84.

[416] Ibid., 86.

[417] Ibid., 91–2 (emphasis mine).

[418] Ibid., 94.

[419] Ibid.

[420] Ibid.

[421] Christine Korsgaard, *The Sources of Normativity*, Cambridge: Cambridge University Press, 1996, 152.

[422] Richard Rorty, *Contingency, Irony, and Solidarity*, 51–2.

[423] Ibid., 39.

[424] Ibid., 62–3.

[425] Ibid., 89.

[426] Ibid., 88–9.

[427] NordForsk, "Interculturalism and Diversities: Developing intercultural models and thinking in the Nordic countries (IDIN)", n.d.a., <http://www.nordforsk.org/en/programs/prosjekter/interculturalism-and-diversities-developing-intercultural-models-and-thinking-in-the-nordic-countries-idin>.

[428] Paul Krugman, "The Times Does Iceland", Blog entry, 8 July 2012, 12:53pm, <http://krugman.blogs.nytimes.com/2012/07/08/the-times-does-iceland/?pagewanted=print>.

[429] Cf. Guðný Björk Eydal and Guðbjörg Ottósdóttir, "Immigration and the economic crisis: The case of Iceland", 2009, <http://thjodmalastofnun.hi.is/sites/thjodmalastofnun.hi.is/files/skrar/immigration_and_the_economic_cri_sis_-gbe_go_strand5_final_1.pdf>.

[430] United Nations and Government of Iceland, "Icelandic Universal Periodic Review. Office of the High Commissioner for Human Rights. Icelandic National Report", July 2011, 14, <http://eng.innanrikisraduneyti.is/media/Skyrslur/Mannrettindaskyrslan---lokaeintak-sent.pdf>.

[431] Cf. Alicia A. Caputo, Stanley Brody and Simon Kemp, "Understanding and Experiences of Cruelty: An Exploratory Report"; and Simon Kemp, Stanley Brody and Alicia A. Caputo, "How Cruel is a Cat Playing with a Mouse? A Study of People's Assessment of Cruelty".

[432] Cesare Beccaria, *Dei delitti e delle pene e Commento di Voltaire*, 42 (translation mine). The different brackets indicate deletions introduced in later editions of his work, trying perhaps to be less controversial.

www.ingramcontent.com/pod-product-compliance
Lightning Source LLC
Chambersburg PA
CBHW061307110426
42742CB00012BA/2093